Now Shall Be Awal

ANTICHRIST

Name
And
Current Location
Revealed

Domenech H.G.

Antichrist, Name And Current Location Revealed:

Endless speculations about the identity of the antichrist have flooded the internet, bookshelves and pulpits across America. Why hasn't anyone thought to look at the Bible itself? Perhaps the answer has been staring us in the face this whole time. The debate is over, the time has come for Christians to see where in the Bible we can find the true identity of the antichrist.

San Antonio, FL 33576 © by Domenech H.G.

All rights reserved. Published 2018.
Printed in the United States of America.

ISBN: 978-0-9996970-1-6

Cover Illustration and Design by Domenech H.G.

Most Scripture quotations from the English Standard Version: where other versions are quoted, those instances are noted.

Contents

Acknowledgements

Glory be to the God of Abraham, Isaac and Jacob…the God of Israel who is also the God that Jesus Christ of Nazareth called his own heavenly father. All Glory and praise and thanks be to that God for he revealed this to me. I alone could have never written this book had God not answered my questions. God showed me the answers and he showed me the light. Jesus Christ of Nazareth is the way the truth and the life and no one comes to the heavenly father except through him. Thank you Jesus Christ of Nazareth.

This book was completed during the two worst years of my life so far. It was seven years of research and chipping away at it but the last two years were so challenging, that I thought this book would never be completed. It wasn't the writing of the book that was challenging. What was challenging was that my family was in a hardship (and still is). Indeed it would not have been completed without the support of my amazing wife Ginger. My children were also enduring every step of the way. Thank you to my wife and kids for supporting me and cheering me on and being my motivation to not give up.

I dedicate this book to Ginger, Nicole, Nadia, Neleia and Nadine.

Intro

Angels had sex with humans. This is obvious in the Bible. Why is it not obvious in the American Church? Why is it not known to probably over 95% of American church members across all denominations? Well this has been hidden for reasons that will be mentioned later in this book but for now lets just say that it is in the Bible. Don't worry, I'm not going to try to convince you of something that's not really true. And the main point of this book is not going to be subject to interpretation. The original ancient Bible is clear. After completing this book, it becomes clear as to why Satan would want to hide that minor little detail about the group of angels that had sex with humans. Most of our pastors, and Bible teachers that have taught us a view that is different than the view of this book are not bad people. Most of those pastors and teachers did not have bad intentions when they told you that the "Sons of God" were human in Genesis 6:1-4.

Understanding who the "Sons of God" are in the Old Testament of the Bible changes the way most of the Bible is understood. But do not worry, the major doctrines that we in America have been taught remain mostly intact. However, many mysterious verses and even entire chapters suddenly become clear. Many things that happened in world history and even today can now be understood. After studying the Bible verses that are analyzed in this book, the Bible (and therefore life) becomes clearer.

The Bible itself will tell you the name and current location of the antichrist. It is not my invention, I will simply show you the verses that God showed me.

Chapter 1

☼ **The Misnomer**

...and they worshiped the beast, saying, "Who is like the beast, and who can fight against it?" (Revelation 13:4, English Standard Version "ESV")

In that verse, the Bible tells us that those that will see the beast with their own eyes will worship that beast and say that there is no one like the beast and that no one can fight against it. Obviously, the beast is therefore, neither Obama nor the Pope (nor Trump, nor Busch). Can you imagine people worshiping Obama to the extent that they feel no one is like Obama and no one can fight against him. There are a large number of MMA fighters that could take Obama down in under fifteen seconds easy. In fact, it rules out a great number of people that have been proposed as candidates to be the 666-beast of Revelation. Many American churches refer to the 666-beast as the "antichrist". More on that later in this book.

Here's a very short Bible quiz;

Pop Quiz:
What are the names of all the books in the Bible that contain the word "antichrist"?

Clue:
The word "antichrist" appears in only two books of the entire Bible.

1

Even if you search by using the ancient biblical Greek word for "antichrist", which is [αντιχριστου] or [αντιχριστος], it still appears in only two books of the Bible (I just gave you a second clue to the pop quiz). While there are several books in the Bible that have significant passages about the end times, there are generally a few that almost always come up in sermons, teachings or discussions about end times prophecies. You almost always hear verses out of the book of Daniel, Isaiah and Mathew chapter 24. But the most notable book in end-times discussions is the book of Revelation. Here are some verses out of Revelation.

Revelation 1:1-3
[1] **The revelation of Jesus Christ, which God gave him to show to his servants the things that must <u>soon take place</u>. He made it known by sending his angel to his servant John,** [2] **who bore witness to the word of God and to the testimony of Jesus Christ, even to all that he saw.** [3] **Blessed is the one who reads aloud the words of this <u>prophecy</u>, and blessed are those who hear, and who keep what is written in it, for <u>the time is near</u>.** (English Standard Version, "ESV")

Revelation 1:19
[19] **Write therefore the things that you have seen, those that are and those that are <u>to take place after this</u>.** (English Standard Version, "ESV")

Revelation is NOT the only book in the Bible containing prophecies of the end times. However, Revelation is clearly the biggest end-times book in the Bible in terms of popularity, content and how often it is quoted in eschatology sermons. Revelation is also the book with the most to say about the mark of the "Beast". The mark of the Beast is the name of the beast and it's also the number of the "Beast". And that number is

666. Revelation also has a lot to say about the Beast itself. Revelation actually reveals a lot about the major players in the end-times prophecies.

So it is not unreasonable for people to include the book of Revelation in the answer to the above pop quiz. But if you answered the pop quiz by saying that Revelation is one of the books where you can find the word "Antichrist", then you might want to take a closer look. The word "antichrist" does not appear in the book of Revelation. In fact, it doesn't appear in the other "big" prophecy books such as Mathew chapter 24.

When I ask Christians the pop quiz question, almost none of them include the books of 1st John and 2nd John. However, those are the ONLY two books in the Bible that contain the word "antichrist". Furthermore, there is no beast anywhere in the entire Bible that is called the "antichrist". There are two different beasts in Revelation that play a major role in the end times prophecies. Neither of those two beasts are ever referred to as the "antichrist" in the Bible. So why then do so many preachers, teachers and evangelists say that the "antichrist" will appear in the end times to rule a one world government and make people get his 666 mark?

Most people include the book of Revelation when they attempt to answer the pop quiz. Most people would expect to find the word "antichrist" in the book of Revelation because that is where you find the verses about 666 and the mark of the beast and lots of end of the world stuff. The word "antichrist" does NOT appear in the book of Revelation, not even one time. Even the English translations of the Bible that are very liberal and very different than most other version do not use the word "antichrist" in the book of Revelation. I have searched in over thirty different English translations and none of them use the word "antichrist" in the book of Revelation. If you find a version of the Bible that uses the word "antichrist" within the book of Revleation, I recommend you get rid of that version of the Bible. That version is tainted and probably with the intent to deceive (or translated by those that were deceived). Replace it with one of the Bibles in the first portion of the list below. Here's a list of the English translations that do NOT use the word "antichrist" within the book of Revelation;

1. King James Version (a.k.a. The Authorized Version)
2. English Standard Version
3. New American Standard Bible
4. The Good News Translation
5. New International Version
6. American Standard Version
7. The New King James Version
8. The Revised Standard Version
9. The New Revised Standard Version
10. 1890 Darby Bible
11. The Contemporary English Version
12. God's Word
13. The Holman Christian Standard Bible
14. Newberry Interlinear Literal Translation of The Greek New Testament
15. International Standard Version
16. Jewish New Testament
17. The Living Bible, Paraphrased
18. Luther Bibel
19. The Message

20. Nestle-Aland Greek New Testament, 27th Edition
21. The New American Bible
22. The New Century Version
23. The New Jerusalem Bible
24. The New Living Translation
25. Young's Literal Translation
26. Wescott-Hort Greek New Testament
27. Amplified Bible
28. Wycliffe Bible
29. World English
30. Weymouth New Testament
31. Tyndale New Testament
32. Jubilee Bible 2000

Later in this book you will find out why this pop quiz question is important. For now I'll just say that the first beast in Revelation, whose name equates to 666 is never called the "antichrist" in the Bible. Furthermore, not even the second beast in Revelation, which causes the world to receive the mark of the first beast, is ever called the "antichrist". Yet most prophecy teachers call the beasts by the title of "antichrist". Why would those evangelists, preachers and teachers call the beast the "antichrist" if the Bible itself never calls the beast the "antichrist".

I've heard credible Bible teachers/preachers say that Obama is probably the "antichrist". Well, Obama himself has admitted to being a Muslim so obviously Obama is one of the billions of "antichrists" that the Bible tells us about. These preachers, evangelists, Bible teachers and others that teach these things have good intentions. There have been some pastors and leaders in my life that I know loved me and cared about me. They had the very best intentions in their sincere heart to teach me the truth about God and the Bible and end-times prophecies. But even though they have the greatest of sincere intentions, they themselves were a victim of the deceit of Satan. I too lived forty years of my life with my blind fold confidently over my eyes. So please do not think that I am condemning nor saying anything bad about those great loving preachers that taught you with honest conviction that Obama might be the "antichrist" or the Pope or the Roman Empire or the Vatican or anything other than what the Bible tells us. The Bible tells us that Satan deceives the whole world.

Revelation 12:09
And the great dragon was thrown down, that ancient serpent, who is called the devil and <u>Satan</u>, the deceiver of the <u>whole world</u>—he was thrown down to the earth, and his angels were thrown down with him. (English Standard Version, "ESV")

Satan has deceived us in so many ways. He has definitely deceived us about the beast whose number is 666. I think this deception is important for Satan because the more we Christians know about the 666-beast the less effective his agenda will be during the coming final days. For the rest of this book I'm going to refer to the main beast as the 666-Beast. It will become increasingly clear as you read this book that the "antichrist" is not the 666-beast...and that the 666-Beast is not the "antichrist". In the Bible there is no such thing as THEE one "antichrist". In other words, there isn't one single main "antichrist". Instead, there are billions of antichrists and the antichrists have been on this planet since the time that Jesus Christ was here on this planet. The only two books in the Bible that use the word "antichrist" are using that word to

6

describe a plurality of people and spirits that do not confess that Jesus is the Christ and people that deny the Father and the Son. Here are the only four verses in the entire Bible that use the word "antichrist".

1 John 2:18
Children, it is the last hour, and as you have heard that antichrist is coming, so now **many antichrists** have come. Therefore we know that it is the last hour. (ESV)

1 John 2:22
Who is the liar but <u>he who denies that Jesus is the Christ</u>? This is the antichrist, <u>**he who denies the Father and the Son**</u>. (ESV)

1 John 4:3
and **every** spirit that does not confess Jesus is not from God. This is the spirit of the antichrist, which you heard was coming and **now** is in the world **already**. (ESV)

2 John 7
For **many** deceivers have gone out into the world, <u>**those who do not confess the coming of Jesus Christ in the flesh**</u>. Such a one is the deceiver and the antichrist. (ESV)

In this book I will identify the 666-beast and his current location based on what the Bible says. I will also show you the verses in the Bible that identify the second beast and his current location. But I first wanted to identify the "antichrist" to get that misnomer cleared up. The four verses above clearly identify the so called "antichrist". Notice the underlined sections and read those parts slowly again. So now you just have to decide, are we going to believe what the Bible clearly tells us or

7

must we bend it a little to make it fit what we've been previously taught. If you decide to believe what the Bible says, then you now realize that the title of this book should really be "*The 666-Beast, His Name And Current Location Revealed*". But then many would probably not be reading this book since most of us have become more interested in the identity of Thee One "antichrist" that Bible teachers told us was coming. Movies have been made about the antichrist, many books written, countless misguided sermons and even special documentaries on the History channel.

To make your understanding of eschatology more clear, you must retrain your mind to think that he ("Thee antichrist") is not coming. Instead, THEY (the many various antichrists) have been here since the first century AD and many more have come since then and many are here today and more to come tomorrow. To understand the bamboozling that is about to happen to this planet, we must stop being on the lookout for the "antichrist" and instead be on the lookout for the beasts that are about to wreak havoc on those that dwell on this planet. Well, that is, if you're trying to be watchful so that you're not blindsided by the arrival of the "antichrist". More important than looking out for the 666-Beast is to be on the lookout for Jesus Christ. That said, however, it is important to become undeceived about the 666-Beast.

Revelation 13:12
He exercises all the authority of the first beast in his presence. And he makes the earth and those who dwell in it to worship the first beast, whose fatal wound was healed.

Sure, you can say that the 666-beast is technically one of the myriad antichrists because he will deny that Jesus is the Christ. But why do you need to continue trying to fit the word antichrist to the 666-beast as if he was thee one antichrist. We should all stop using the word antichrist in eschatological discussions because by using that word, we continue to feed the confusion and promote the inaccurate idea that the one single antichrist is coming. Indeed there are two main beasts that are coming and in this book we will get to the bottom of it. By the end of this book, you will know where in the Bible the name of the 666-beast is revealed and where the Bible says that he is currently located. The Bible also tells us the name and location of the second beast and this book will point you to those verses as well. However, a few more pieces to the puzzle must be put into place before a clear picture begins to emerge.

Chapter 2

☿ **Who Controls This World**

This is one of the most important chapters in this book. Hang in there as I unfold a very key fact without which most of this book is hard to grasp. Without a clear understanding of the point of this chapter, you might get lost trying to understand today's important current affairs here in the US as well as worldwide. In fact, even much of the Bible is hard to grasp without understanding the point of this chapter. In this chapter I will show you Biblical evidence hidden within the very Bible that you own (well, it's not really hidden rather it's overlooked and inadequately taught in most American Christian Churches). I will also reveal more modern and shocking evidence outside of the Bible and in the world that we can currently observe.

With all the evil and wickedness in this world, it's a valid question to ask who's actually in control of this wretched world we live in. The following list is not to condemn anyone, since we were all born sinners. I don't feel like I'm holier nor better than another Christian. I struggle with sin too. Thank God for Jesus Christ and the salvation that can only come from the death and resurrection of Jesus Christ. So the purpose of this list is to point to the fact that this world has a staggering amount of evil in it.

- 45% of marriages are expected to end in divorce.
- 70% of men have cheated on their wife.
- 25% of girls were sexually abused in 2015. Many of those girls were under the age of ten (10).

11

- 20% of boys were sexually abused in 2015.
- 79% of adult bisexual women were sexually molested when they were minors.
- Only 2% percent of rapist serve time.
- Over 25 million Americans used an illegal drug in 2013.
- 41,000 Americans died of illegal drug overdose in 2015.
- 437,000 worldwide were intentionally and illegally killed in 2012 not including military operations.
- 13 billion dollars were spent on pornography in 2006 in the U.S..
- Due to the amount of free pornography on the internet, global pornography revenue has decreased by 50% from 2007 to 2015.

That's just a very short list of all the evil in this world. In light of that list, it should not be so hard to believe the Bible when it says that Satan is the ruler of this world. That is not a typo in this book. I actually said that the Holy Bible calls Satan "The Ruler of This World". In fact, the Bible says that the "evil one" is in control of this whole world. Do not be afraid, us Christians are going to be saved and we'll be just fine. I'm not inventing a new doctrine. I'm just revealing one that has been hidden from you and your parents and your grandparents for thousands of years. It has been hidden from many pastors, Bible scholars, teachers and evangelists.

But this will be hidden from you no longer for I am about to reveal it to you. Well, actually, I feel like there's no possible way I could have uncovered all of this without God somehow revealing it to me. One Christian plants the seed another

Christian waters it, but God causes the growth. Next we'll take a look at some of the Bible verses that tell us who the ruler of this world is and who controls this world and who has the authority in this world. After that, we'll look to see if we can find any physical evidence outside of the Bible in the physical modern world that we currently live in. After all, if Satan does control this whole world, there might be some evidence somewhere (especially if you search hard enough). Let's begin our search in the Bible for the answer to the question of who is the ruler of this world and therefore currently in control of this world.

Revelation 13:2-4
²And the beast that I saw was like a leopard; its feet were like a bear's, and its mouth was like a lion's mouth. And to it **the dragon** gave **his power and his throne and great authority**. ³One of its heads seemed to have a mortal wound, but its mortal wound was healed, and the whole earth marveled as they followed the beast. ⁴And they worshiped **the dragon**, for **he** had given **his** authority to the beast, and they worshiped the beast, saying, "Who is like the beast, and who can fight against it?"
(ESV)

To unpack these three verses a bit, let's take a closer look at this dragon mentioned in verse 2 and verse 4. Who is this dragon? This dragon is Satan of course. We confirm that the dragon is Satan by reading Revelation 12:9.

Revelation 12:9
And **the great dragon** was thrown down, that **ancient serpent**, who is **called the devil and Satan**, the deceiver of the whole world—he was thrown down to the earth, and his angels were thrown down with him. (ESV)

13

In a different chapter in Revelation, we see additional confirmation that this dragon is actually Satan (there are more than one significant dragon in ancient biblical history as well as in non-Biblical history).

Revelation 20:2
And he seized the dragon, that ancient serpent, who is the devil and Satan, and bound him for a thousand years (ESV)

So now we know that one of the dragon's is Satan in the book of Revelation. We just saw that Revelation chapter 13 tells us that the dragon gave his power and his throne and great authority to the beast. If Satan did not have a throne, power and GREAT authority, how could Satan give that to the beast. That of course could not happen unless Satan had great authority to give in the first place. Chapter 13 in Revelation is not trying to teach us that Satan has a throne with power and great authority. It assumes that the reader already knew about Satan having a throne with great power and authority. You see, when John (the writer of Revelation) wrote this, he already knew that the twelve apostles of Jesus Christ had previously been taught about Satan's throne, power and great authority. In the first century A.D., the Apostles had heard Jesus refer to Satan as "the ruler of this world". In the following verses of the Bible, the Apostles did not stop Jesus to ask him, "Jesus, why do you call Satan the Ruler of this world". It was probably ancient Israelite tradition to teach that Satan was the ruler of this world. Those 12 Israelites who became the 12 Apostles already knew from ancient Israelite teachings of the Old Testament. They had prior knowledge of Satan's authority, power and throne. This knowledge of Satan was handed down through oral tradition and rabbinic teachings. Additionally,

Jesus probably taught the apostles the details surrounding the throne of Satan, power of Satan, and authority of Satan.

Now let's look at the Gospel of Luke. We've all had someone teach us or read to us about Luke chapter 4. Many of you have read Luke chapter 4 a few times. This time we will read it in slow motion so that we can notice something that usually gets passed up and somehow ignored in Bible teachings (especially in the Christian churches in America). I'm not trying to bash churches in America. I love, love, love the Christian congregations but we need to start feeding some meat to our congregations (the milk is good but the time has come for Christians to grow in the word). Here's Luke in slow motion.

Luke 4:5-7
And the devil took him up and showed him all the kingdoms of the world in a moment of time, ⁶ and said to him, "To you I will give all this authority and their glory, for it has been delivered to me, and I give it to whom I will. ⁷ If you, then, will worship me, it will all be yours." (English Standard Version, "ESV")

This pericope is mentioned in three of the four Gospels. It tells us about when Jesus Christ was fasting for 40 days and 40 nights out in the wilderness. At the end of the 40 days of fasting, Jesus was tempted by the devil.

- Mark 1:12-13
- Matthew 4:1-9
- Luke 4:1-13

Notice in Luke that Satan and Jesus are talking to each other. In the Gospel of Luke, Satan is called the "devil" but we know that the devil is another name for Satan in this excerpt because the devil says that all the kingdoms of the world have been delivered to him (i.e. all the kingdoms of the world have been delivered to the devil). Here we see that the devil is the one that is offering to give all the authority to Jesus Christ. The devil says to Jesus that the devil can give the kingdoms and the authority to anyone that the devil wants to give it to. If you feel like I just found a typo in the Bible, don't worry. Everything in the Bible is still true. I am NOT trying to teach new doctrines. Jesus is still the only begotten son of God and Jesus is still our only savior. In the end, Satan loses all the power and authority and Satan loses control of this world. Halleluiah! Remember that we just saw in Revelation that in the end times, Satan gives his own throne, power and authority to the beast. Therefore, two thousand years ago, the devil did NOT give all his kingdoms of the world nor all his authority to Jesus.

At this point in the story, in which Satan is tempting Jesus, it would seem like an obvious response from Jesus might be for Jesus to say to Satan something like "...what are you talking about Satan, have you lost your mind, you of all people know good and well that I Jesus am the one who has the throne and the power and the authority over all the kingdoms of the world". The Bible tells us the response from Jesus. Satan tells Jesus that if Jesus will worship Satan, then Satan will give all authority and the glory of the kingdoms to Jesus. They both knew each other very well. At the time of this temptation, Satan and Jesus had known each other for at least thousands of years before Jesus was manifested through a human birth through the Virgin Mary. Jesus did not begin his existence two thousand years ago when he was born through the Virgin

16

Mary. Jesus is an eternal God and Jesus and his heavenly father YAHWEH are the creators of all things. Jesus created the Garden of Eden and Jesus created Adam and Eve. Jesus was co-creator working closely with his heavenly father YAHWEH. Take a look at John chapter 1.

John 1:1-3
In the beginning was the **Word**, and the **Word** was with God, and **the Word was God**. ²He was in the beginning with God. ³**All things** were made through him, and **without him was not any thing made that was made**. (ESV)

In the book of Genesis, anything that was created in the beginning was created through Jesus Christ. In John chapter 1, Jesus is called the Logos which is Greek for Word. Jesus is the Logos (i.e. Jesus is the Word). How can we confirm that John chapter 1 is referring to Jesus when it says "Word". Lets take a look at verses 14-15 to confirm that chapter 1 is talking about Jesus and that chapter 1 calls Jesus the "Word"

John 1:14-15
¹⁴ And **the Word** became flesh and dwelt among us, and we have seen his glory, glory as of **the only Son from the Father**, full of grace and truth. ¹⁵John bore witness about him, and cried out, "This was he of whom I said, 'He who comes after me ranks before me, because he was before me.'"

So then, Jesus and Satan go way back with much history between them. I'm sure that Jesus loved Satan very much before the fall of Satan. Before Satan was called "Satan" he was probably called by a different name (e.g. possibly the light bearer or Lucifer). Since Satan knew exactly who he was tempting in Luke, it would have been a meaningless and stupid thing for Satan to tell Jesus that Satan had the authority over all the kingdoms, if it was not true. It might sound like a husband telling his wife that he was the one that birthed their child. If you're not yet convinced that Satan is in control of this world and that Satan is the ruler of this world, then let's look at other verses in the Bible.

John 16:11
and in regard to judgment, because **the prince of this world** now **stands condemned**. (NIV)

In John 16:11, Satan is called "the prince of this world". In some English translations (e.g. NASB, ESV, and others), Satan is called "the ruler of this world" in John 16:11. This verse makes it harder to deny that Satan is indeed the ruler of this world because it says that he "now stands condemned". Well, right there we know that the Bible isn't talking about Jesus being "the ruler of this world". But still, I know this is a tough pill to swallow so here's another verse that might help.

John 14:30
I will no longer talk much with you, for **the ruler of this world** is coming. **He has no claim on me**, (ESV)

Some Bibles have red color font to highlight the words of Jesus himself. John 14:30 (as well as John 16:11 above), are in red color font in those Bibles because these are the words of Jesus Christ himself. Jesus calls Satan the ruler of this world and since it is Jesus talking here we know that he's not talking about himself. Furthermore, Jesus says that the ruler of this world has no claim on me. Why would Jesus say that Jesus has no claim on Jesus? Or why would Jesus say that his heavenly father has no claim on Jesus. Almost every person that I present this to struggles to believe that Satan is in control of this whole world. Therefore, we'll take a look at yet another verse on this matter.

John 12:31
Now is the judgment of this world: now shall <u>the prince of this world be cast out</u>. (King James Version, "KJV")

In the above verse, the King James Version calls Satan "the prince of this world". Other English translations such as ESV, NASB, Amplified Bible, International Standard Version and others have it as "ruler" instead of "prince". Looking at multiple English translations can often be helpful in gaining a better understanding of certain words. Notice that this verse says that "the prince of this world" will "be cast out". In some Bibles, the above verse is in red colored font so we know that it is Jesus doing the talking in this verse (even if your Bible doesn't have red font, you can still clearly determine that Jesus is doing the talking because of the context...just start reading in the prior chapter and read through). We know that Jesus is not saying that Jesus will be cast out. So who is it then that will be cast out. It is the prince of this world that will be cast out, not Jesus. If you claim to believe the Bible, then you now must believe that Satan is the prince of the world, the ruler of this world and the one in control of the whole world. But if you still struggle to believe this...

1 John 5:19
We know that we are children of God, and that the <u>whole world</u> is under the <u>control of the evil one</u>. (New International Version, "NIV")

Here's the part of this book where some people just throw their Bible away. Some people simply refuse to believe that Jesus Christ is NOT the ruler of this world (at least currently, he's not). It is human nature to reject very disturbing facts. Sometimes we simply write them off as some nonsense or some glitch in the interpretation system. How many times does the Bible have to say it before you believe it? Well, for some of you it's enough already but please bear with me because I know some of you are still rejecting this Biblical fact. The following verse, in 2 Peter chapter 1, reminds us that it does NOT depend on how YOU interpret it. It is a lie from Satan that scripture can be interpreted differently depending on how you read it.

2 Peter 1:19-21

[19]And we have something **more sure**, the prophetic word, to which **you will do well to pay attention** as to a lamp shining in a dark place, until the day dawns and the morning star rises in your hearts, [20]knowing this first of all, that **no prophecy of Scripture comes from someone's own interpretation**. [21]For no prophecy was **ever** produced by the will of man, but men spoke **from God** as they were carried along by the Holy Spirit.

If you were Satan, wouldn't you want humans to think that Bible verses can have several different meanings depending on how each individual interprets it? That's a brilliant thing that Satan has achieved. Because now that many have been deceived to think that scriptures are flexible and bendable in their meaning and the extent to which they are flexible is up to you, then Satan can suggest some things that seem acceptable just like he suggested some things that seemed acceptable to Adam and Eve. With that level of elasticity, any verse can take on practically any meaning that you need it to. We tend to make the Bible verses stretch until they match up with our preexisting belief system. Now I do agree that it is possible for Bible verses to have different LEVELS of meaning but ALL the levels are perfectly aligned such that they have no hint of contradiction with each other.   The Bible does NOT contradict itself.

Basically, at this point, you have to decide that you either believe that Satan is the ruler of this world or you have to admit to yourself that you don't really believe the Bible. Or maybe some people just prefer to stretch it and shape it until it fits more comfortably. But if you believe the Bible is the word of God, it's too clear to deny it.

If you're a true Bible believer, then we have seen enough verses and now you know that Satan is the ruler of this world and he controls the whole world and he currently has the authority over all the kingdoms of the world. You who believe the Bible do not need to see additional evidence outside of the Bible. But for those of you who don't fully trust the Bible, we'll take a look at some hard evidence found outside of the Bible that matches up with what the Bible says. This extra biblical evidence helps prove the case that the Bible has it right.

The following facts (which occurred after the Bible was written) help to prove that the Bible is true. This has been hidden from you by secret societies and esoteric groups. Since it has been hidden so well, you'll need to follow closely as I build each piece of the puzzle for you. If you type the words "satanic symbol" into an internet search engine, you will find the following symbol comes up a lot in several flavors. This is known as the pentagram.

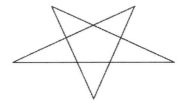

Another version is the pentagram within a circle like this.

The pentagram has that horizontal line and the star has a single point at the six o'clock position. It usually has two horns. The point of the top horns are located very roughly around the ten and two o'clock position. The pentagram is called a pentagram because of the prefix "PENT", which means five. There are five main angles pointing outward from the center of the pentagram. In the occult (or satanic organizations), the pentagram is sometimes depicted with the head of the goat.

The occult teachings are ancient and these esoteric ideas have their origin in the Garden of Eden starting with Adam and Eve. I'm sure you recall what Genesis says about the ideas that Satan introduced to Eve (see Genesis chapter 3). Today, Satan and his myriad brigades and divisions require their human worshipers to keep things secretive or die. Indeed they sell their soul to the devil. In exchange for worship and loyal devotion to Satan, the humans in global leadership positions are promised power and wealth. Success is also promised to industry leaders and the top decision makers in every important institution of society (e.g. the financial system, military, international affairs, healthcare, insurance, energy, media, education, entertainment, and everything of any significance and literally the whole world). Does Satan really have secret schemes?

Exodus 8:6-7
⁶So Aaron stretched out his hand over the waters of Egypt, and the frogs came up and covered the land of Egypt. ⁷But the magicians did the same by their <u>secret</u> arts and made frogs come up on the land of Egypt (ESV)

2 Corinthians 2:11
in order that Satan might not <u>outwit us</u>. For we are not unaware of his <u>schemes</u>. (NIV)

Ephesians 6:11
Put on the whole armor of God, that you may be able to stand against the <u>schemes</u> of the devil. (ESV)

Jude 4
For certain persons have crept in <u>unnoticed</u>, those who were <u>long beforehand</u> marked out for this condemnation, ungodly persons who turn the grace of our God into licentiousness and deny our only Master and Lord, Jesus Christ. (New American Standard Bible, "NASB")

Notice in Jude 4 above that the bad guys crept in unnoticed. Where did they creep into? They have crept into high positions of power and influence within the organized Christian churches here in the US (and world wide). They started creeping in during the first century as members of those congregations. And Satan has helped them to work their way into the inner core of the corporate offices of most of our major Christian denominations today. I'm talking about all the big name denominations. Some of the leaders of our largest Christian denominations do not even know that they have been deceived. As they read this paragraph, they are confident that I'm not talking about them (that is an example of deception).

Chapter 3

⛧ Evidence That Satan Is The Ruler

Satan has maintained an unbroken continuity since the time of Adam and Eve. Even after the flood, Satan and his brigades of fallen angels have continued forwarding Satan's agenda with the help of some humans. In every century of human history, Satan has had certain handpicked humans working closely with him so that Satan could advance his agenda through these appointed humans. Around the 13th century (A.D.), there was one human that was known at the time to enter into pacts with Satan himself. He was a known Satanist, magician, conjurer, and necromancer known as Dr. Faust. He called himself Georgius Sabellicus. Efforts have been made to erase his true history and even make him out to be a fictitious character that never existed. This is partly because he was paid by German aristocrats to conjure up the devil and other powerful fallen angels. The devil and his fallen angels helped the German aristocrats to gain power and wealth through knowledge and special favors. However, we know he existed for several reasons. He earned his doctorate degree in divinity in 1509 from Heidelberg University. Furthermore, there were too many complaints about his demeanor. Several complaints were filed about him searching through cemeteries and digging up corpses. Dr. Faust called himself the prince of necromancers. Several writers have written about Dr. Faust making him increasingly legendary. Dr. Johann Georg Faust lived from approximately 1460's to 1540's and was from the area of Knittlingen, Württemberg. But this is not a book about Dr. Faust. He is, however, an important piece to this chapter

25

because one of the famous plays about his dealings with the devil reveals to us something very key. It helps us to find the evidence of who controls this whole world and who is the ruler of this world.

The occult and esoteric teachings are transferred to initiates in secrecy. That secrecy is one of the reasons that we know very little about the satanic symbols. Some symbols we've never even seen before. I don't recommend to anyone that they go seeking out the mystery teachings of the various Satanic organizations. I went searching after I decided to leave the Christian church and it nearly cost me my eternal life. I never got initiated nor did I do any of the rituals. I never did any of the acts that they're known for such as sacrificing nor anything like that. The most I did was read and study and read and study because curiosity got the best of me. I just wanted to know what the secrets were that were being kept from me. But I strongly urge you to avoid falling for any temptation and do NOT go reading about Satanism or the occult.

There is one thing, however, that I must reveal to you. There is one symbol that I think is important for you to know about and I think you'll agree. This secret satanic symbol is revealed in one of the occult plays written about Dr. Faust and his dealings with the devil. The following excerpt is from a play written by Johann Wolfgang von Goethe. This section is from the play, "Faust Part I".

<u>Faust:</u>
>So you set the Devil's fist
>That vainly clenches itself,
>Against the eternally active,
>Wholesome, creative force!
>Strange son of Chaos, start

26

On something else instead!

Mephistopheles ("Devil"):
Truly I'll think about it: more
Next time, on that head!
Might I be allowed to go?

Faust:
I see no reason for you to ask it.
Since I've learnt to know you now,
When you wish: then make a visit.
There's the door, here's the window,
And, of course, there's the chimney.

Mephistopheles ("Devil"):
I must confess, I'm prevented though
By a little thing that hinders me,
The Druid's-foot on your doorsill

Faust:
The **Pentagram** gives you pain?
Then tell me, you Son of Hell,
If that's the case, how did you gain
Entry? Are spirits like you cheated?

Mephistopheles ("Devil"):
Look carefully! It's not completed:
One angle, if you inspect it closely
Has, as you see, been left a little **open**.

Faust:
Just by chance as it happens!
And left you prisoner to me?
Success created by approximation!

Mephistopheles ("Devil"):
The dog saw nothing, in his animation,
Now the affair seems inside out,
The Devil can't get *out* of the house.

Faust:
Why not try the window then?

Mephistopheles ("Devil"):
To devils and ghosts the same laws appertain:
The same way they enter in, they must go out.
In the first we're free, in the second slaves to the act.

Faust:
So you still have laws in Hell, in fact?
That's good, since it allows a pact,
And one with you gentlemen truly binds?

Mephistopheles ("Devil"):
What's promised you'll enjoy, and find,
There's nothing mean that we enact.
But it can't be done so fast,
First we'll have to talk it through,
Yet, urgently, I beg of you
Let me go my way at last.

Notice the word "pentagram" in that play. We saw earlier in this chapter that the pentagram is a satanic symbol which has five main angles which are the five points of the star. In this play about Dr. Faust, the devil is called "Mephistopheles". The devil meets with Dr. Faust and then the devil asks for permission to leave the house. Dr. Faust is surprised that the devil asked permission to leave. The devil then confesses that the pentagram (a.k.a. "the druid's foot") is preventing the devil from leaving because one of the angles of the pentagram is a "little open". The following is what a pentagram looks like with one angle left a "little open".

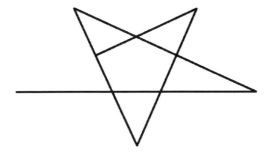

Regardless of whether it is true or not, the pentagram with one angle left open represents (to the Satanist) the power to hinder Satan's ability to leave once the occultists conjures him up (or at least some level of influence on Satan). I do not know if any humans can have any influence on Satan's ability to leave. I suspect that Satan has deceived those humans into thinking that occultists might be able to hinder Satan or have any level of influence over Satan. I even suspect that it is not even Satan himself that shows up when magicians and conjurers call up Satan. I suspect that it's possible for Satan to have other powerful fallen angels show up to pretend to be Satan. In my research, I found extremely strong evidence that at least some humans have successfully communicated with Satan himself. All speculation aside however, these humans that are occultists, magicians and Satanists are convinced that certain symbols, words, rituals, sacrifices, incantations and other behavior can lead to power, wealth and other benefits.

It is no secret that the White House in Washington DC is one of the most powerful places in the world. One thing that is a secret, however, is that Satan controls the White House. Here's a short list of some of the decisions and actions that start in Washington DC and affect the whole world.

- Major laws are established
- Wars are declared
- Citizens and other entities are taxed
- Social Security Numbers are issued & monitored
- Monetary policy implemented
- Health care policy is determined (e.g. "Obamacare")
- Education standards are established
- Other countries are subjected to trade embargos, taxes, tariffs and other economic policy
- News and other media is controlled by the FCC
- Trade (i.e. buying and selling) is controlled by the FTC
- The entire world depends on decisions made in the White House

In Washington DC, there is a lot of evidence of Satan hidden in symbols, images and architecture. Go to www.google.com/maps (or any other map of DC) and take a close look at the layout of Washington DC. Especially, notice what sits **ABOVE** the White House as you look on a map (i.e. North of it). It's a pentagram with one angle left a "little open". Here is what the street map looks like from the sky (turn your book sideways for proper orientation of North and South).

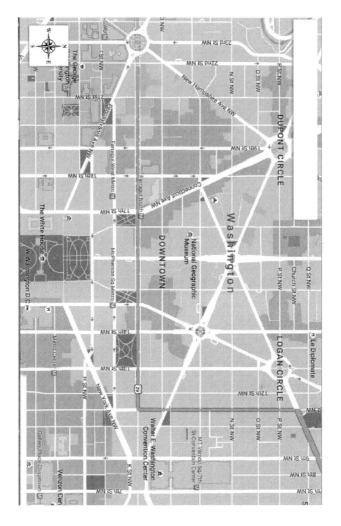

Notice the White House at the bottom of the map (South end) and towards the center of the image. You'll need to turn the book such that the White House is at the bottom of the image. The next image shows the same map but with the five points of the pentagram highlighted in black. The center of each circle marks the point of each star. The Eastern most point of the star is marked by a rectangle with the point being located at the center of that rectangle. The Southernmost point of the star is marked by the White House such that the White House has a pentagram siting immediately North of it. In other words, the head of the goat is resting its chin on the White House. This highly secretive occult symbol was constructed around 1792 in Washington DC, therefore, we ought not blame the current presidents and leaders for they had nothing to do with it.

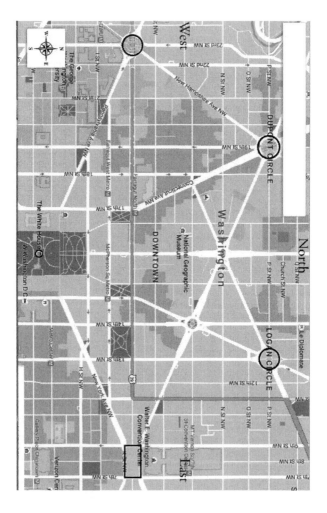

Now it should be easier to see the pentagram with one angle left a "little open".

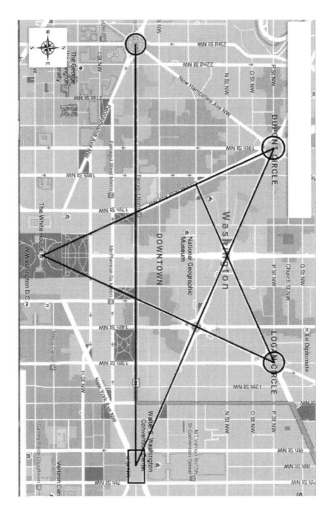

Below is the pattern that emerges immediately North of the White House and perfectly aligned with the White House with regards to the four cardinal directions (i.e. North, South, East, West).

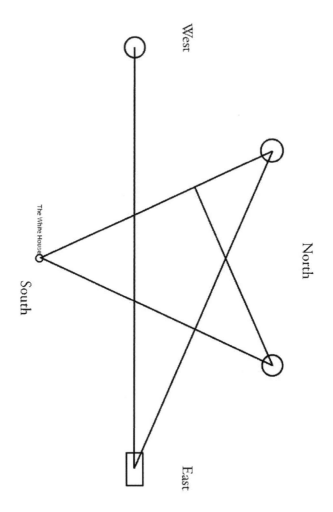

West

North

The White House

South

East

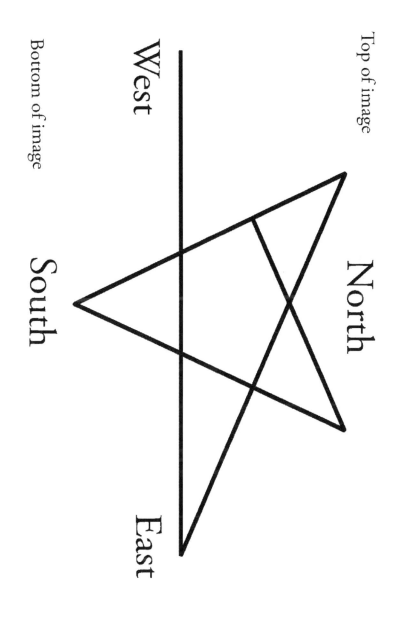

Top of image

West

Bottom of image

South

North

East

35

So now you have two sources of evidence pointing to the fact that Satan is the ruler of this world and therefore controls the whole world. The pentagram (with one angle left "a little open") that sits immediately North of the White House is a pretty good piece of evidence. However, there is so much more evidence as you look through the symbols, icons, and pagan architecture that adorns Washington DC. Where in Washington DC do you see a federal monument or federal building that makes the statement that Jesus Christ is our savior? Nowhere! There's not even one clue in DC that would indicate Jesus Christ as our savior. (As I type this paragraph, I feel a welling up inside of me that makes me want to scream at the very top of my lungs that Jesus Christ is my savior and I worship him and his heavenly father for that). But even if you ignore all the modern day evidence and write it off as coincidental, you still have to deal with the fact that the Bible calls Satan "the ruler of this world" and says that the whole world is under the control of the evil one. So if you ignore all the evidence around us, it leaves us with only one question...do you really believe what the Bible says? Or is it more comfortable and more convenient to just pick and choose the nicer parts of the Bible and just believe those parts. Earlier in this chapter we looked at six (6) different verses in the Bible that tell us that Satan has authority and power over this whole world. How many times does the Bible have to say it before it's true?

The fact that Satan is the ruler of this world must be fully digested and understood before we're able to understand how it has been possible for Satan to keep us in the blind about the 666-beast. Once Satan's authority, power and rulership becomes clear to you, it will become possible to perceive and discern the identity and current location of the 666-beast (more popularly known as "the antichrist"). However, most Christians will find the Bible hard to believe.

Revelation 12:09
And the great dragon was thrown down, that ancient serpent, who is called the devil and Satan, **the deceiver of the whole world**—he was thrown down to the earth, and his angels were thrown down with him.

The above verse clearly tells us that Satan is the deceiver of the whole world. It's hard to find an English translation of the Bible that does not say "<u>the whole world</u>". I was fully deceived for the first forty (40) years of my life. Now I am less deceived but I'm sure there are still things that Satan has hidden from me. He was able to deceive our parents, our grandparents, our great grandparents and many other ancestors. But thanks to the God of Abraham, Isaac, and Jacob, God is opening my eyes little by little. Praise be to the God of Israel who is the heavenly father of Jesus Christ.

Indeed there were probably many Christians that came to America as explorers, pilgrims and settlers. However, the Christians did not come alone. Others with greater financial backing and support came along with the Christians. Satan deceived some of those more resourceful men. He helped the "founding fathers" to quickly gain control of the newly re-discovered America.

So anyway, everything (nearly everything) important that you've been taught about history is wrong. That includes the history of America (from the re-discovery of America to the founding of America to this very second in which you read this), ancient history, pre flood history, medieval history, and much of all the other events in History. Why, because a liar must create other lies to cover up the original lies and lies on top of lies are required to keep it all under cover. Satan is the liar according to the Bible. As much as we'd like to think that Satan's lies don't affect us Christians, they do…they affect us very much in our everyday lives. It takes some time to digest all of this because the lies and deceit are very significant and have very deep far reaching implications.

When I introduce the evidence in this book to Christians, most of them have an initial reaction of aggressively rejecting it. The hair stands up on the back of their neck, they turn red and almost teary eyed. I even saw one co-worker swell up with fear and she began to turn red and it seemed like she was struggling to swallow a very large lump. Most people respond to me with some sort of defensive wording indicating their rejection of the evidence I present to them. But really, the thing that they are rejecting is the Bible. I showed you the verses now you just have to decide if you believe the Bible or not. Don't blame me for the shocking surprise because I didn't start the fire…it was always burning since the world's been turning (some of you caught that).

Later in this book, you will see why it is important for Satan to keep secret the identity of the 666-beast and to keep secret the location of the 666-beast. Even after this book is published, most Christians will remain deceived about the 666-beast. This is because Satan controls the whole world which includes control of the media and control of major book publishers and control of major corporations and much much more…in fact, the Bible says he controls the whole world. It staggers me how people that claim to believe the Bible refuse to understand that the Bible is trying to tell us that Satan controls the WHOLE WORLD....Hello, is there anybody out there. But, but, but, but...no, there is no but. It is the whole world that Satan controls. And the reason some of us struggle to believe this part of the Bible is because Satan saw us coming. Long before our grandparents were born, Satan knew that he'd have to set up an education system that would gradually direct the minds of the people toward a mindset that would make it nearly impossible for us to see the truth...even if the truth was written in the Bible. Even if the truth was blinding you in the face, you'd still have a hard time believing it. How slick that Satan is.

Chapter 4

Sons of God Were Not Human

This chapter examines the Hebrew manuscripts of the Bible to clarify an often obscured Bible fact. Many scholars agree that a strong technique for Bible study is to interpret scripture with scripture. That tool will be used to help answer the question of who are the "Sons of God" as mentioned in Genesis 6:2-4. Most Bible scholars fall into three main groups with regards to who they think the "Sons of God" are in Genesis chapter 6. One group believes the "Sons of God" (in Genesis) are the sons of Seth who is a human mentioned in Genesis 4:26. In this discussion, that group will be called "The Sethites". Another group believes that they are the sons of human kings that were followers of God and, therefore, "godly sons". In this book, the people that believe that will be called "The Kingites". The other main group believes that the "Sons of God" (in Genesis) are NOT human but rather supernatural beings which some refer to as heavenly beings, heavenly host or angels.

Keep in mind that words can have completely different meanings when just one single letter or punctuation is changed or added. Following are some examples of this.

Table 4.1	
Cares	Caress
Needles	Needless
Car	Care
Car	Scar

Table 4.2	
Scar	Scare
Tear	Team
Pain	Paint
Lean	Clean

Words can even have different meanings without any letters changing. In such a case the definition of the word is determined by the context. Following are some examples of that.

Table 4.3
Bear: the animal; or to hold up or support
Pound: unit of currency; or hit with force
Solution: solving a problem; or homogeneous mixture
Tear: to pull apart with force; or the natural eye fluid

Furthermore, to better understand the context of a word found in the ancient manuscripts of the Bible, one must also study the culture and other social implications of the time and location of the specific book being studied. Keep in mind that there exists dozens of attempts to translate the Bible into English. Why dozens? One reason is because Bible scholars disagree as to what the words really meant. If they agreed, there would be one version in the English language. The disagreement could simply be a result of newly unearthed manuscripts (e.g. Dead Sea Scrolls) or other new archeological findings. Newly discovered paintings, carvings or even entire cities have been found in modern times. Another reason for different interpretations of the same manuscript is because some words in the ancient manuscripts simply do not exist in English. Therefore, scholars working on interpretations must try to choose between a few English words that might all be somewhat close candidates in some way or another (but not exact).

The word elohim is a transliteration of a word found in the ancient manuscripts. To transliterate a word is simply to write it in a way that most closely resembles the pronunciation of the word rather than the meaning. The word elohim is an arrangement of letters from the English alphabet rather than an actual English word. The word elohim did not exist in the English language until people attempted to pronounce the Hebrew word by using English letters. There is no word in English that has the same exact meaning as the Hebrew word that is pronounced elohim. The Hebrew word (אלהים) which is transliterated as elohim is found over 3,000 times in the Old Testament books including Psalms 82:6-7, which reads as follows.

Psalms 82:6-7

⁶I have said, Ye are **gods**; and all of you are children of the most High. ⁷But ye shall die like **men**, and fall like one of the princes. (KJV)

The above two verses are the words of God the father who is also the most high god and the one that many call Yahweh (the God of Abraham, Isaac and Jacob). He is also the only God worshiped by the author of this book, in the name of Jesus Christ.

In Psalms 82:6-7 (quoted above), who is Yahweh speaking to when he says "Ye" and "You"? The word "But" in verse seven is a clue to answer this question. Another clue is how that word "But" is translated in other English versions. Following are other English translations of the same verse.

Psalms 82:6-7

⁶I said, "You are gods, sons of the Most High, all of you; ⁷nevertheless, like men you shall die, and fall like any prince." ("ESV")

Psalms 82:6-7

⁶I said, "You are gods, And all of you are sons of the Most High. ⁷Nevertheless you will die like men And fall like any one of the princes." (New American Standard Bible, "NASB")

In English, the word "nevertheless" is like saying "in spite of that" and the word "but" functions to introduce something that is in contrast with what was just previously said.

Therefore, what Yahweh is saying to the gods (who are also sons of the most high) has the following meaning when using the word "nevertheless"; *In spite of the fact that you are all gods and in spite of the fact that you are all sons of the most high, you will still die like human beings die.* The reason there is contrast is because angels[1] were initially created as eternal beings that cannot die (Luke 20:36). When using the word "but", it has the following meaning; *You are all gods and you are also sons of the most high God, however, in contrast to that fact, you will still die like humans die.* It would not make sense for someone to say the following statement; You are a human being but you will die like a human being. That statement would be a useless waste of ink, leather, parchment or papyrus.

Writing supplies were not regarded in the same way we now view a pack of printer paper containing 500 sheets for $5 or $6. When God sent us his holy word, each and every single letter was selected with great care to convey meaningful things of the highest importance to humanity. Therefore, Psalms 82:6-7 conveys an important truth which is that Yahweh himself is clearly stating that the sons of the most high (his own

---

[1] All elohim are non-human. There are different types of elohim. Some elohim are angels but not all elohim are angels. Some elohim are cherubim, seraphim, messengers, archangels and the most high is an elohim.

44

sons) are gods. And those verses also shed light on the fact that these sons of the most high God are NOT humans. It just stands to reason that the sons of God would be gods. That they are not humans is confirmed by the presence of the word "but" (or "nevertheless") which functions to express the contrast between the phrase that precedes the word "but" and the phrase that follows the word "but". It is recommended that readers of this book take a look at these two verses in the Biblical Hebrew language. Following is how Pslams 82:6-7 is written in the ancient manuscripts. The Autograph's didn't have those little dots above and below the letters. Furthermore, the Autographs were more than likely written in pictograph characters (e.g. Aleph would have been the actual head of the ox or bull).

⁶ אֲנִי־אָמַרְתִּי אֱלֹהִים אַתֶּם וּבְנֵי עֶלְיוֹן כֻּלְּכֶם:

⁷ אָכֵן כְּאָדָם תְּמוּתוּן וּכְאַחַד הַשָּׂרִים תִּפֹּלוּ:

Notice that in verse six, the ancient manuscripts have the word elohim (אֱלֹהִים) which is highlighted above. In ancient cultures, the word elohim was never used in reference to humans because everyone knew that elohim were not human. Overtime, however, society evolves and cultures allow words to drift a little in their definition. Eventually it can drift so far from its true original meaning that it can actually have opposing meanings like the word "bad". There was an era around the 1990's where the word "bad" could mean "good" or even better than "good". People would say things like "the paint job on that race car is bad" but the meaning was that the paint job was excellent or awesome. In the days when the word "bad" originated, it was never used to mean "good". Another

45

example is the word "cool". For most of its existence, the word cool was strictly about temperature and never once used to mean something "hip" or "excellent".

In contrast to the word elohim, in verse six is the word kadam (כְּאָדָם) in verse seven above, which means Adam or human. Psalms is a collection of writings by various men of God over a period of about a thousand years from 16th century BC to about 6th century BC. In the times when Psalms was originally written, no one used the word elohim in reference to humans because they all knew that no elohim was human. Over time and especially after the resurrection of Jesus (begining around 70 AD), various influences have caused the word elohim to slightly expand. However, just because some modern thinkers need the word elohim to have a more elastic definition does not mean that the original meaning of God's word changed. People in history create different denominations and variations of doctrines not necessarily because they have bad intentions. Sometimes a well-meaning pastor or scholar has been the victim of deceit (and they might not yet realize it). This deception creeps in because our struggle is not against flesh and blood humans. Instead, our struggle and battles are with the invisible beings which are principalities, rulers and powers of the dark side (Ephesians 6:12). It makes sense that Satan and his band of fallen angels would want to implement a strategy that would cause as many as possible to think that they don't even exist. It would also make great strategic sense to cause as many humans as possible to be unaware of the fact that fallen angels had sex with humans (this book will show why).

The word elohim appears 3,180 times when searching for that exact sequence of letters within a single word in the Biblica Hebraica Stuttgartensia ("BHS"). Although not perfect, the BHS is one of the authorative Hebrew texts of the Old Testament. The Enhanced Strong's Lexicon ("ESL") says the word elohim occurs 2,606 times in the Old Testament (it can not occur in the New Testament since the NT manuscripts that are available are in Greek). The difference between a digital search and the ESL is attributed to the occurrences in which the word elohim has other letters attached to it such as the letter "L" in the word lelohim (לֵאלֹהִים). According to the ESL, the word elohim is translated to the word god 99.4 percent of the time (or 2,590 times out of 2,606). However, the word elohim has a different definition than the word "god" (or at least different than how most Americans would define the word "god"). The reason that the word "god" is used by translators is because there is no single word in the English language that has the same exact meaning as the word elohim. Following is a compiled summary of how the most authoritative dictionaries and encyclopedias of the Biblical Hebrew language define elohim;

ELOHIM (אלהים): *Celestial non-human beings that are from the supernatural realm, the highest and most powerful of which is Yahweh the creator of all other elohim. Elohim existed before planet earth was created. In ancient times (before Jesus Christ), elohim were divine beings.*

That definition is from the perspective of the ancient Israelites that subscribed to the orthodox Jewish beliefs. It includes what Americans today call angels. Technically, however, there are different types of non-human spirit beings.

Some should be called messengers, watchers, seraphim, cherubim, archangels or other terms rather than categorizing them all as angels. With that understanding, it makes more sense when the Bible says "the most high god" (Gen 14:18-22; Psalms 78:56; Daniel 3:26; Daniel 5:18; Daniel 5:21). The very fact that the Bible sometimes refers to Yahweh as "the most high god" should make one realize that there are other gods that are not as high. If there were no other gods, then those verses that say "most high god" would be like saying that the Niagara Falls is the most tall of all the Niagara Falls in New York. If there is only one elohim, then there is no need to say that he is the highest elohim. That phrase ("the most high") implies that there are others in that special league of beings. The matter of whether the word elohim is singular or plural is similar to that of the word "fish". It would not be correct to add the letter 's' to the word fish in order to make it plural. Whether the word "fish" is plural or singular is determined by the context and so it is with the word elohim. By itself, the word elohim is in the plural form which means that it naturally defaults to a plural definition. However, the context in the Bible is almost always singular and so it is almost always translated as god rather than gods.

The Dead Sea Scrolls ("DSS") have been used to confirm and clarify some of the English translations of the Bible (for the Old Testament). However, the DSS were not found until 1947 (long after the original King James Version). The DSS were not published (and thus not available) for Bible translators to use until 1991. This means that all English translations that were created before 1991 did not have the benefit of the DSS for the Old Testament ("OT"). The English translations before 1991 relied mostly on the

Masoretic manuscripts with the oldest one being from the 9th century AD. These Masoretic manuscripts are compiled into the Biblia Hebraica Stuttgartensia ("BHS"). One of the most significant contributions of the DSS is the clarification of Deuteronomy 32:8. Following is how that verse reads in the English Standard Version ("ESV") Bible.

Deuteronomy 32:8-9
⁸When the Most High gave to the nations their inheritance, when he divided mankind, he fixed the borders of the peoples according to the number of the sons of God. ⁹But the LORD's portion is his people, Jacob his allotted heritage.

The DSS were written sometime between the first century BC and the first century AD. The DSS are one of the most significant finds in human history. The clarification of this one verse alone (Deut 32:8) by the DSS is worthy of an entire book but that is not the focus of this book. Until the DSS were available to Bible translators, there was debate as to how this verse should be translated. Some believed that this verse should say "Sons of God" while others thought it should say "Sons of Israel". A Masoretic scribe changed Deuteronomy 32:8 to say "Sons of Israel" instead of "Sons of God" for theological reasons. The fact that it was changed by that scribe was forgotten and assumed by many American congregations to be correct until the DSS were released. After studying the DSS, it was no challenge for scholars working on English translations to accept verse 8 as saying "sons of God". It is easy to accept this for several reasons and one reason is because it is how the Septuagint has it (the Septuagint is the major Greek translation of the OT created by seventy Jewish Rabbis during the 3rd and 2nd century BC). Another reason is because many foggy things about human history suddenly become clear. For example, why are there so many ancient cultures that worshipped so many different gods? And why are there so many different ancient cultures with similarities in their religious beliefs? Some translations are even clearer and show it as "angels of God" instead of "sons of Israel" in Deuteronomy 32:8. The DSS have it as "Sons of God" which is why the following English translations do not use the word "Israel" in verse 8. Instead of "sons of Israel", below is a table showing how some English Bibles translate that part of verse 8.

Table 4.4 (Deuteronomy 32:08)	
Name of Bible Translation	How It Is Translated
English Standard Version-ESV	Sons of God
New English Bible-NEB	Sons of God
Revised English Bible-REB	Sons of God
The New American Bible-NAB	Sons of God
The Revised Standard Version-RSV	Sons of God
The New Revised Standard Version-NRSV	the gods
The New Living Translation-NLT	angelic beings
The Message	divine guardians
The Good News Translation-GNT	heavenly being
The Contemporary English Version-CEV	guardian angel

After completion of this book, the definition of "Sons of God" in the OT will be clearer. For now, notice that five of the above translation teams made it clear that Deuteronomy 32:8 is not talking about humans. The other five chose not to use the word Israel and you can rest assured that those translators knew that "sons of God" are not human to many Bible readers.

The fact that "sons of God" in Deuteronomy 32:8 is not about the twelve tribes of Israel and thus not the "sons of Israel" becomes obvious when looking at the context of verse 8. Here is the quote with verse 7 included.

Deuteronomy 32:7-9
⁷Remember the <u>days of old</u>; consider the years of <u>many</u> generations; ask your father, and he will show you, your elders, and they will tell you. ⁸When the Most High gave to the nations their inheritance, when he <u>divided</u> <u>mankind</u>, he fixed the <u>borders</u> of the peoples according to the number of the sons of God. ⁹But the LORD's portion is his people, Jacob his allotted heritage. ("ESV")

In verse 8, when did Yahweh "divide mankind"? Verse 7 gives a clue as to when that division took place and it happened in "the days of old" and "many generations" prior. This division of nations involved fixing the borders. The above Bible quote is referencing back to the Tower of Babel event described in Genesis chapter 11. At the time of the Babel event, the "sons of Israel" did not yet exist. The twelve sons of Jacob were not born until centuries after the Tower of Babel event. Verse 8 talks about "THEIR" inheritance while verse 9 talks about "the Lord's portion".

At the tower of Babel event, Yahweh gave the humans over to fallen angels and put one fallen angel as king over each nation except the nation of Israel. I use the phrase "fallen angel" only because most readers are more familiar with that phrase rather than "the lower gods". However, those "fallen angels" are actually the lower gods. In Deuteronomy, the Lord himself is the king of Israel. So the nations are "THEIR" inheritance (the fallen angels' inheritance) while the Lord's portion is the nation of Israel (i.e. the 12 tribes of Israel). I did not invent this idea of each ancient nation having a king over it that was a fallen angel. The Dead Sea Scrolls confirm that the "beney ha elohim" were given the position of king over each nation. So there were seventy[2] fallen angels in charge of every nation in the world except Israel. One "beney ha elohim" per nation. This helps to explain the tradition of the ancient Mayan ruins (and ancient Egypt and so many ancient civilizations). It also helps to explain the phenomenal ancient architecture that baffles modern man. For example, unexplainable pyramids and megalithic structures with precision that only one century ago was impossible to modern humans. The "beney ha elohim" are not originally from this planet since they witnessed the creation of this planet. That makes them aliens to planet Earth. They're aliens by the dictionary definition not by the "Hollywood" definition. Research will turn up more information on Deuteronomy 32:8 for the readers.

One reason to discuss this is to point out why some believe that the "sons of God" in Genesis are human kings and rulers. The angels (a.k.a. "sons of God") were indeed kings and rulers and so were some of their hybrid human offspring (the heir to the throne). Those half human half angel Nephilim are also known as demi-gods. This all started at the Tower of Babel event when Yahweh set all the national borders according to the angels and gave the disobedient people over to the fallen angels. All nations, except Israel, had at one point a fallen angel as their king. And the heir to the thrones of those nations were the

---

[2] There is some evidence that points to 72 nations instead of 70.

hybrid offspring of the angels. Examples of these hybrid kings are Og, Anak, Abimelek and kings of Cannan.

Understanding who the "Sons of God" are in the Old Testament of the Bible changes the way most of the Bible is understood. But do not worry, the major doctrines that we in America have been taught remain mostly intact. However, many mysterious verses and even entire chapters suddenly become clear. Many things that happened in world history and even today can now be understood. You and me as Christians are "CHILDREN" of God and the Bible says we have the right to become "SONS" of God. You and I as Christians will become co-rulers with Jesus and he will share his throne with us after we become "sons" of God. Until then, we are children of God. The distinction between a "child" of God and a "son" of God is not the subject of this book and that distinction deserves an entire book. It is in the Bible and it becomes clear with careful study of the actual Bible. After studying the Bible verses that are analyzed in this book, the Bible (and therefore life) becomes clearer.

There are ONLY six (6) times in the entire Old Testament ("OT") in which the Hebrew phrase בני האלהים occurs. That is pronounced as "beney ha-Elohim". One of those six times (Job 38:7), the Hebrew letter ה is omitted in which case it reads as בני אלהים. In that verse, it would be pronounced beney elohim. In the other five verses, the Hebrew letter ה serves the same purpose as the English word "the". So it's kind of like saying "sons of the God" instead of "sons of God". The word "*the*" was omitted in all six verses when scholars translated them into English versions of the Bible. That's because these six are considered to be the same by scholars that interpret the

Bible into English.   There are 12 times in the Old Testament where one or more beings are referred to as a son of God using any number of different phrases.   Below is a list of these 12 verses divided into two separate tables.

Table 4.5			
Verse	**Hebrew**	**English**	**Note**
Job 38:7	בני אלהים	Sons of God	non humans ("angels")
Job 1:6	בני האלהים	Sons of God	non humans ("angels")
Job 2:1	בני האלהים	Sons of God	non humans ("angels")
*Deut 32:8	בני האלהים	Sons of God	non humans ("angels")
Genesis 6:2	בני האלהים	Sons of God	non humans ("angels")
Genesis 6:4	בני האלהים	Sons of God	non humans ("angels")

*For Deuteronomy 32:8, see Table 4.4 in this chapter for a list of Bible versions that have it as "sons of God".

Table 4.6

Verse	Hebrew	English	Note
Psalm 82:6	בני עליון	sons of the most high	non-humans
Daniel 3:25	לבר־אלהין	son of god (son of the gods)	non-humans
Hosea 1:10	בני אל חי	Sons of the living god	Humans can be "children" of God. After atonement by Jesus, humans have the right to become sons of the living god
Deut 14:1	בנים אתם ליהוה אלהיכם	you are the children of the lord your god	human Israelites
Psalm 29:1	בני אלים	sons of might	non-humans

The main thing to take away from the two previous tables is that the only time ("beney ha-elohim") is found in the manuscripts it is always in reference to non-humans. Notice the exact sequence of letters in Table 4.5. Look at the first four verses in Table 4.5. In all four of those occurrences, all the authoritative Bible commentaries agree that beney ha-elohim are non-humans. For the last two Bible verses in Table 4.5, many of today's Bible scholars consider the "sons of God" to be non-humans as well. But the last two verses in Table 4.5 are the only two verses out of those six that are in dispute among scholars today. However, after completing this book, it will be clear that in ancient Biblical times, the phrase "beney ha-elohim" was reserved for non-humans every time. There is absolutely nothing in the ancient Hebrew manuscripts that

55

even slightly supports the belief that the "sons of God" in Genesis 6:4 are humans. The scholars making the argument that the "sons of God" in Genesis 6:4 are humans, are simply trying to hang on to their pre-existing believes. It is simply human nature that makes it difficult for people to let go of things that were taught to them by their well-meaning pastors, professors, parents and other loved ones. It is very uncomfortable to accept the possibility that something so game changing has been misunderstood by so many respected authorities. While it is good to protect and regard the Bible as sacred, it is also good to realize that a deeper understanding is possible. The loved ones that have taught our culture did not have bad intentions. They were not trying to deceive their congregations, their children and their students. They truly believed that their teaching was correct. However, no human teacher can be more correct than the Bible itself.

Chapter 5

What Did It Mean In Hebrew

How can it be that something so profoundly revolutionary can be misunderstood by so many pastors, professors, scholars and experts? One explanation of why millions of church members across America are not aware that angels had sex with humans is found in the Bible. Ephesians 6:12 tells us that our struggle in life is not against human beings. Instead, our struggle is against the elohim that have fallen out of Yahweh's grace. The fallen elohim (a.k.a. fallen angels) have good reason to try to deceive the humans. Another reason is that we were brought up in a very different culture compared to the culture of Moses. The differences in culture, language and society make it difficult to fully understand all the nuances of those ancient Biblical writings. However, seek and ye shall find. The Holy Spirit of God will help us. And in the end times, knowledge will increase (Daniel 12:4).

Consider the hypothetical situation in this paragraph, for example. Imagine if everyone in the whole world vanished and disappeared forever except for ten people left on this planet. The only ten people existing in this planet are now from a primitive tribe deep in the Amazon jungle who only understood a very rare dialect. They start roaming the world and eventually they make their way to what use to be the United States of America. There they began to figure out how to read the books in English and eventually they figure out the meaning of the words warm and cool. After the primitive Amazonians realize that the word "cool" refers to temperatures, they eventually encounter a sentence in a magazine that reads as follows; "that sports car is so cool". The Amazonians might spread the teaching that the sports cars are not warm temperature wise. Language issues like this existed in ancient times. Over three thousand five hundred years (3,500) have passed since Moses was told what to write in the Torah. Imagine how disconnected we are today from ancient idioms. Think about idioms like "he kicked the bucket".

A wise Rabbi once said, "the English language does not convey Hebrew thought". The English language has many conceptual words whereas the ancient Hebrew is more connected with tangible things such as a river, a branch of a tree, a tent, a seed, or any number of tangible things that everyone can easily connect with. This is largely why English cannot convey Hebrew thought.

Idioms are not the only problem that translators have when they attempt to translate the Bible. There are ancient euphemisms, ancient metaphors, ancient metonymies, homonyms and a whole litany of translation problems resulting from the cultural, theological and social differences. One of many examples of a word that causes translation problems is in Genesis 26:8. The word is (מְצַחֵק). That word is translated into the following words depending on which English Bible translation you look at;

Table 5.1	
Caressing	Amplified Bible
Making Love	The Living Bible, Paraphrased
Fondling	The Message
Making Love	The Good News Translation
Laughing	English Standard Version
Sporting	American Standard Version
Caressing	New American Standards Bible
Caressing	New International Version
Sporting	King James Version

Genesis 26:8
When he had been there a long time, Abimelech king of the Philistines looked out of a window and saw Isaac <u>laughing</u> with Rebekah his wife. (ESV)

As is often the case, the context helps to understand verse eight. Notice verse nine.

Genesis 26:9
So Abimelech called Isaac and said, "Behold, she is your wife. How then could you say, 'She is my sister'?" Isaac said to him, "Because I thought, 'Lest I die because of her.'" ("ESV")

Here is the same verse in the KJV.

Genesis 26:9
And Abimelech called Isaac, and said, Behold, of a surety she is thy wife: and how saidst thou, She is my sister? And Isaac said unto him, Because I said, Lest I die for her. ("KJV")

The Bible says Abimelech looked out the window and saw Isaac doing "something" with his wife and in the very next verse Abimelech comes to the sure conclusion that she is Isaac's wife. Moses wrote that Abimelech looks out the window and as a result of what Abimelech saw he confronted Isaac and said for sure she is your wife so why did you say she is your sister. Whatever Abimelech saw when he peeked out the window convinced Abimelech that she must not be his sister but obviously his wife. So he probably didn't see them laughing or sporting, but probably more like fondling, making love or caressing her in way that one would not caress his sister.

Another translation problem is the personal beliefs of the translators and other influences. The King James Version ("KJV") was not what Moses (nor the Apostles) were told to write. That should be obvious because they were not given English words to write. Acts 12:4 is just one piece of evidence of this. Notice the word Easter in that verse. Easter was never celebrated in the actual Bible. That verse should say Passover NOT Easter. The word Easter occurs only one time in the entire KJV. And the word Easter never occurs in the ESV, NIV, NASB, ASV nor the other major translations. If you do enough research you'll find evidence that Easter is a pagan holiday not a Christian one. And if you don't have time to do the research, just ask yourself how the bunny and the colored eggs became such a big part of a supposedly "Christian" holiday. And at which point in history did the rabbit and eggs enter into the tradition? The translators of the KJV probably did not have bad intentions to deceive you. More than likely it was just an error in the translation caused by some infiltrating influence. Or maybe our struggle is not against flesh and blood (cf. Ephesians 6:12). And, certain people have crept in unnoticed to pervert the grace of our God (cf. Jude 4). Between Ephesians 6:12 and Jude 4, it should not be hard to believe that the word Easter was sneaked in to the King James Version. I know some of you have been taught that the King James Version is the ONLY version that is good but you better look into this Easter verse more closely because you can rest assured that those Jews were not celebrating Easter in Acts 12:04. They were celebrating Passover NOT Easter. Another example that shows the translation errors in the KJV is found in 1 John 2:20 which reads as follows;

1 John 2:20
But ye have an unction from the Holy One, and ye know all things. ("KJV")

Have you ever met a human being that knew ALL things? That verse (1 John 2:20) is written to the fathers, sons and children that were mentioned earlier in that chapter in verses 14 & 18. Those believers did NOT know all things because God the father is the one that knows all things. But do not worry, I'm not suggesting that you throw away your King James Version, just keep in mind that it is a "version" of the attempted English translations and not the actual Bible itself. The actual Bible itself was written in ancient Hebrew and Ancient Greek (although it is possible that the New Testament autographs might have also been written in ancient Hebrew and or Ancient Aramaic).

When the English Bible reads as "Sons of God", the Hebrew letters that appear in the actual Bible (ancient Hebrew bible) are בני האלהים which means "Sons of God" or "Sons of Elohim" or "members of Elohim". Elohim means God. Other occurrences use different Hebrew letters because in those verses it uses different words (i.e. Sons of the Mighty,

61

Sons of the Most High). But in all eight verses, the Bible is clearly talking about a select group of individuals known as the SONS of God the Almighty Creator...so whoever we uncover these individuals to be (those SONS), they are the sons of the almighty creator of all things.

The New Testament is different than the Old Testament because not only was it written in a much different time with different writing traditions and different cultural meanings but also because the copies of the New Testament were written in Greek and Aramaic, which are entirely different languages. Therefore, it would be an error to use the words "Sons of God" from the New Testament. It would be an error because we're trying to figure out how that term (Sons of God) was used in ancient times before the New Testament was written.

Following is an analysis of the eight verses that lead to an understanding of who the "Sons of God" are in the Old Testament. The New American Standard Bible is quoted below but you can find the words "Sons of God" in all other popular English translations such as the NIV or King James and others. So the analysis turns out the same regardless of which translation you use.

Job 1: 6-7
⁶ Now there was a day when the sons of God came to present themselves before the Lord, and Satan also came among them. ⁷ The Lord said to Satan, "From where do you come?" Then Satan answered the Lord and said, "From roaming about on the earth and walking around on it."

In the above verse, notice that Satan came along with the "Sons of God" to negotiate before God. It should be clear that humans were not coming up to God (with Satan among them) to present themselves. Satan is the leader of a band of fallen angels known (in ancient times) as the "Sons of God" (all angels were called "Sons of God" whether good or bad). Also, the word angel should really be "spirit being" in this discussion because there are different classes/types of spirit beings and some were called angels, while others were classified by other words (e.g. cherub, seraphim, principalities, powers, watchers, messengers, angels, etc). Whether or not it was good angles or bad angels (that Satan came with that day) is irrelevant for this analysis because we simply want to know just who the "Sons of God" are in the Old Testament. Clearly these were spirit beings ("angels") and not humans. Humans simply can't physically walk into the presence of God accompanied by Satan and on their own free will and present themselves to him (no human can see Gods face and live…and a human had to be behind a veil or curtain). And why would Satan come among humans to approach God. Further studies show that no serious Bible scholar has ever thought that the "Sons of God" in this verse were not angels (all serious scholars agree, at least in this verse).

Job 2: 1
¹ Again there was a day when the sons of God came to present themselves before the Lord, and Satan also came among them to present himself before the Lord.

Above is a different verse in the book of Job (a different chapter), where we see once again that Satan comes with the "Sons of God" to present themselves to God in an attempt to negotiate. Satan comes AMONG the "Sons of God" so this cannot be humans for only spirit beings or "angels" would have traveled with Satan like that (Satan was a spirit being). But the spirit beings could materialize into bodily form and touch humans and interact with them.

Job 38: 4-7

4 "Where were you when I laid the foundation of the earth? Tell Me, if you have understanding, 5 Who set its measurements? Since you know. Or who stretched the line on it? 6 "On what were its bases sunk? Or who laid its cornerstone, 7 When the morning stars sang together And all the sons of God shouted for joy?

In the above four verses, which is an excerpt from a discourse between God and Job, there's an obvious reference to the time of the creation of the world. In this context, the "Sons of God" refers to what we call angels, which are created spirit beings. This is always the case where the expression "Sons of God" occurs in the Old Testament. Who else could have been there to witness the creation of the world? God is asking Job...where were you when I created the earth and the Angels sang together and shouted for Joy. The "Sons of God" witnessed the creation of the earth but Job did not. It is a well-known and agreed fact that angels are often called stars and in this case are called "morning stars" (actual stars do not sing).

Daniel 3: 25 & 28

25He said, "Look! I see four men loosed and walking about in the midst of the fire without harm, and the appearance of the fourth is like a son of the gods!" . . . .
. . . . . 28Nebuchadnezzar responded and said, "Blessed be the God of Shadrach, Meshach and Abed-nego, who has sent His angel and delivered His servants who put their trust in Him, violating the king's command, and yielded up their bodies so as not to serve or worship any god except their own God.

In the above section in the book of Daniel, King Nebuchadnezzar sees a fourth man in the fire furnace that he says is like a "son of the gods" and then in verse 28 (three verses later) and in the same context he says that God sent his "angel" to deliver Shadrach, Meshach and Abed-Nego. So Nebuchadnezzar refers to the angel as a "son of the gods". It's interesting to note that most of the popular English versions of the bible translate it as gods with an 'S' but the King James version translates it as 'God' without the plural 'S'.

Psalms 82:6
⁶I said, "You are **gods**, and all of you are sons of the Most High.

When the above verse says "you are gods", it is obviously not talking about humans. In ancient times, some thought of angels as gods. In the above verse, a reading of the chapter of Psalms 82 makes it undisputable that the "Sons of The Mighty" in this verse are clearly angels and cannot be human. All Bible scholars agree to that, in this verse. This verse should be enough to make it clear for you...if not, just read it again very slowly.

Psalms 89:6
⁶For who in the skies is comparable to the Lord? Who among the sons of the mighty is like the Lord,

In the above verse, the context is those that are in the skies. Humans are not in the skies. A reading of the chapter of Psalms 89 makes it undisputable that the "Sons of The Mighty" in this verse are clearly angels and cannot be human. Bible scholars agree to that, in this verse also.

Genesis 6: 2
² that the sons of God saw that the daughters of men were beautiful; and they took wives for themselves, whomever they chose.

In the above verse, the actual Bible (in Hebrew) uses the Hebrew words that mean "human girls" which is translated as "daughters of men". The word human is used by the author of Genesis to make a clear distinction between human and non-humans because the Sons of God are not human, they are angels which are spirit beings created by God before he created humans. This verse says that the angels took human wives for themselves. Which, by itself, does not mean they had sex with them....just that they took them as wives.

Genesis 6: 4

⁴ The Nephilim were on the earth in those days, and also afterward, when the sons of God came in to the daughters of men, and they bore children to them. Those were the mighty men who were of old, men of renown.

In the above verse, Nephilim is the ancient Hebrew word for the hybrid offspring resulting from an angel having sex with a human female. Angels are not Nephilim. Only their hybrid offspring are Nephilim.

In the preceding 4 pages we looked at the eight verses, which mention the "Sons of God" in the Old Testament;

1. Job 1:6-7
2. Job 2:1
3. Job 38:4-7
4. Daniel 3:25,28
5. Psalms 82:6
6. Psalms 89:6
7. Genesis 6:2,
8. Genesis 6:4

One of those 8 (Gen 6:4) does say that the angels had sexual intercourse with the human daughters and that the human daughters bore them children. The mighty men of old who were men of renown are the gods of Greek mythology. Greek mythology originated from stories passed down from the Hitites. And in turn the Hitites received the tradition from an even older civilization called the Hurians.

Chapter 6

☼ **What In The Hell**

1 Peter 3:19

[19] in which also He went and made proclamation to the spirits now in prison, [20] who once were disobedient, when the patience of God kept waiting in the days of Noah, during the construction of the ark, in which a few, that is, eight persons, were brought safely through the water.

The spirits that are in prison in verse 19 are the same spirits that were disobedient in verse 20 above. They are not human, they are spirit beings which existed before the creation of planet earth. These are fallen angels that disobeyed by fornicating with humans as well as other disobedience.

2 Peter 2:4-5

[4] For if God did not spare angels when they sinned, but cast them into hell and committed them to pits of darkness, reserved for judgment; [5] and did not spare the ancient world, but preserved Noah, a preacher of righteousness, with seven others, when He brought a flood upon the world of the ungodly;

Above, we see that the angels sinned before the flood and were put into a prison (the prison is located here on earth underground…see Greek word "Tartarus").

Jude 6-7

[6] And angels who did not keep their own domain, but abandoned their proper abode, He has kept in eternal bonds under darkness for the judgment of the great day, [7] just as Sodom and Gomorrah and the cities around them, since they in the same way as these indulged in gross immorality and went after strange flesh, are exhibited as an example in undergoing the punishment of eternal fire.

In verse seven above, the word "they" includes Sodom and Gomorrah as well as the cities around them. The word "these" are the angels of verse six. This is demonstrated by a Biblical Greek expert below (Dr. Wuest). And remember, there are no verse numbers in the actual Bible.

The Greek word for abode in Jude 6 is οἰκητήριον (oikētērion). This word can mean a couple of things but one of the definitions in the Greek dictionary is (the tangible body inhabited by a spirit). That Greek word is also used to mean the type of imperishable body that humans will indwell with their spirit in heaven.

1 Corinthians 15:39
39 For not all flesh is the same, but there is one kind for humans, another for animals, another for birds, and another for fish. 40 There are heavenly bodies and earthly bodies, but the glory of the heavenly is of one kind, and the glory of the earthly is of another. ("ESV")

This abode is the spiritual body that angels have in heaven but the fallen angels abandoned not only their domain but also the special body which housed their spirit in Heaven. They were disembodied. God didn't use two different words (i.e. "domain" & "abode") just to improve the literary value of his writing. He used two different words because God was talking about two distinct and separate things. The "domain" is the region of the universe (or the realm) that they were located, which in this case was in the presence of God himself. And then the word "abode" which is the tangible tent that houses their spirit. Just like we humans are a spirit that possesses a flesh and blood tent. It is possible that angels in heaven do not have sex while they are in that special oiketerion. But when they come here to earth, some are able to become disembodied and

70

then somehow materialize into a flesh and blood human like body (I mean maybe…I'm just saying that many reasonable explanations might exist). You can find several instances in the Bible where angels performed functions of a flesh and blood body like eating with men or getting their feet washed or physically touching humans. One angel even cooked a meal for a human. And many times in the Bible there are angels that look exactly like humans and are even mistaken as humans. The bible says you can entertain angels without even knowing it. The homosexuals of Sodom & Gomorrah wanted to have sex with the Angels that they saw at Lot's house (see Gen 19:4-8).

The following verse provides further proof that Angels had offspring.

Genesis 3:15

15 And I will put enmity between you and the woman, And between your seed and her seed; He shall bruise you on the head, And you shall bruise him on the heel.

In the above verse God is speaking with Satan. Satan is called a serpent and a dragon in other books of the Bible. And Jesus is called a lamb and a lion. But Satan is no more an actual snake than Jesus is an actual lamb. So God is not talking with an animal but rather an angel (i.e. an elohim). God is talking with a fallen angel who was called Lucifer ("light bearer") and is now called Satan (and Satan is also called a serpent…see revelation). In the above verse, God said "**YOUR** seed" when talking to Satan. Satan's seed is the offspring of Satan. Seed is used to mean offspring in the Bible. Why would God talk about the offspring of Satan if angels cannot have offspring? Because there's nothing anywhere in the Bible that says angels cannot have offspring....not even one verse. Read the above verse slowly. Does it say "the seed of evil men"? NO. Does it say "the seed of those that worship Satan"? NO. It says "YOUR seed". It would be erroneous to assume that God is talking about anything other than the seed of Satan himself. Do not try to make the Bible mean what you've always been taught that it means. Let the Bible mean what it actually says.

Who in the Old Testament was worthy of being called a "Son of God"? Would you say Noah, or Abraham, or Moses, or Daniel or Job...who was worthy? None of those humans were even one time called a "Son of God" in the Old Testament. Not even Enoch who walked with God was called a "son of God". No one except elohim (non-humans) were called "son's of God" in the Old Testament.

But in the Bible, there's a verse that is used by evil spirits for the purpose of trying to cover their tracks. The evil one distorts the perception of the following verses. The following single verse doesn't provide sufficient detail to come to the conclusion that it is physically impossible for angels to have sexual intercourse with humans. Yet that is what some believe. They point to when Jesus says the following... "For in the resurrection they neither marry nor are given in marriage, but are like angels in heaven.". Those words of Jesus are found in the gospels and repeated in three of the Gospels (Matthew 22:30, Mark 12:25, Luke 20:35). But if you read the chapter, you'll notice that Jesus is addressing the question of which of her seven dead husbands does the widowed woman belong to when she gets to heaven. They didn't ask Jesus who the woman will be able to have sexual intercourse with....only the question of belonging.

Here is additional proof that the word "marriage" in the bible does not mean sexual intercourse.

Revelation 19: 7 & 9
[7] "Let us rejoice and be glad and give the glory to Him, for the marriage of the Lamb has come and His bride has made herself ready." . . . . . . [9] Then he said to me, "Write, 'Blessed are those who are invited to the marriage supper of the Lamb.' " And he said to me, "These are true words of God."

The above passage in the Bible is talking about the coming marriage between Jesus and the people of God. The above two verses in Revelation should be sufficient proof that Marriage does not mean sexual intercourse. But even though this biblical evidence is undisputable, some will still insist that the bible says that angels are physically incapable of having sexual intercourse even if angels leave their proper abode and manifest bodily here on hearth.

Is it physically possible for someone to have sexual intercourse with someone that they're not married to? Yes it is. Therefore, the word marriage doesn't have the same definition as the word fornication or intercourse.

Is it physically possible for someone to never have sex with their spouse? Yes it is.
Therefore, marriage is not the same thing as sexual intercourse. This is not asking if they WOULD completely avoid sex, rather is it physically possible to avoid sex.

Furthermore, consider the following questions;

1) Once we get to heaven, will angels there murder some of us? No they will not. But they are physically capable of doing that when they are on earth.

2) In heaven, might angels deceive some of us and cause us to worship angels instead of God? No they will not...but they have the skill and ability to do so when they are on earth.

3) Might angels in heaven steal from us or murder us when we get there? No they won't...but they have the skill and ability to do so when they are on earth.

4) For the above questions, is it physically possible for them to do the above things... which is different than will they or do they? There is a very big difference between the two.

5) So the question of whether they do or don't is a different question than whether it is physically possible or impossible...is it not?

Jesus didn't say that it was physically impossible for angels to have sex. Because he wasn't even addressing sex. And even if some think that Jesus was addressing sex, he was addressing what they don't do in heaven just like they don't murder humans in heaven and just like they don't deceive humans in heaven. It is possible that humans will not have sex in heaven (perhaps because it is unnecessary or undesirable...maybe there's something better than sex...and maybe heavenly bodies are capable of something much greater than sex). And whatever the reason is for that, maybe there would also be a similar reason why angels can physically have sex on earth but not in heaven. He was using the example of what angels don't do in the resurrection not what angels don't do on earth (the resurrection is clearly different than earth and the body we'll have in the resurrection is clearly different than the current flesh and blood body, because Luke 20:36 says we can't even die anymore).

Also, it is possible that Jesus was indicating that angels don't marry each other...but that doesn't address whether or not angels can have sex with humans...maybe angels don't have sexual intercourse with angels.

It is clear that angels (being supernatural spirit beings), can transform out of the unseen spirit realm into a touchable and physical flesh and blood form. Therefore, it's also possible that the flesh and blood form is unnecessary in heaven.

Do not add words or change a word or subtract a word from the bible. Read what it actually says and try to understand each word in it's context....the words are "marry / marriage" not "sex"

In Conclusion, the analysis of the Old Testament is clear. Anytime the words "Sons of God" appear in the Old Testament, it refers to spirit beings ("angels") that are not human but rather spirit beings created before the earth was created (this applies to "Sons of the Most High" or "Sons of the Mighty"). Whether they are good angels or bad angels depends on the verse, but regardless, they are angels (good or bad) never humans. Furthermore, the "Sons of God" were able to get human females pregnant resulting in the birth of giants which appear throughout the bible. In the bible, these giant offspring of the fallen angels are called by various names including Nephilim, giants, Rephaims and Anakims. Nephilim means Giants (or a flesh and blood offspring lacking the original human DNA because one of the parents or grandparents was an elohim, or "Angel"). Rephaims and Anakims are clan names of different Nephilim groups. Goliath was over 6 cubits tall.

The word cubit is the name of a unit of distance (e.g. inch, foot, meter, centimeter, etc). The exact distance of a Cubit depends on which civilization, which social group and which era. Cubit refers to the distance from the tip of the elbow to the farthest outstretched finger (i.e. the length of an arm). The arm of a giant was much longer than the arm of the Israelites. And therefore has a different interpretation depending on the context but the ancient Hebrew cubit is about 24 inches making Goliath over 12 feet tall. The ancient Hebrew cubit is not 17 to 19 inches like some bible interpreters believe. The common cubit of a human was somewhere between 17 to 19 inches. The author of this book has an arm length of about 19 inches (from elbow to tip of middle finger). The fallen angels (and their offspring) have made great effort to hide the giants from us. Private museums currently have skeletons of giants that are 12 to 15 feet tall. Some skeletons have been found that are over 15 feet tall. The same dark deceivers that have obscured the fact that the fallen angels caused human females to give birth to giants has also caused the true size (and even the historic existence) of these giants to be a guarded secret.

For thousands of years, and up until 40 years after the resurrection of Jesus, no one in history ever attempted to dispute the fact that the "Sons of God" in the Old Testament were angels. Until 70 AD, it was common knowledge worldwide that angels were called "Sons of God". Even in other ancient world religions there are stories of "gods" mating with humans to yield demigods. Prior to 70 AD, every culture, every nation, every religion and every society knew these powerful spirit beings as either "Sons of God" created by God or actual gods (in their mind). Why did Jesus not set the record straight about these "Sons of God" while he walked this earth...he surely must have heard others talking about it on occasion. Why wasn't it until ~40 years after his resurrection (70 AD) that the interpretation began to change. Wouldn't have Jesus corrected everyone during his walk on earth in the first century. Why would Jesus continue to allow people to call these spirit beings the "Sons of God". And why would he continue to allow people to believe that these spirit beings fornicated with humans to create the giant offspring. Both of the most highly regarded historians of the 1st century clearly acknowledge the fact that angels mated with humans to yield giant offspring (see Josephus and Philo). I suspect that Jesus didn't set the record straight for his apostles because everyone in his time already knew about the elohim having sex with humans. No one in history ever debated this topic until 70AD when the fallen angels (the ones that weren't imprisoned) along with their offspring began their campaign to obscure this fact by deceiving some influential humans so that they would begin to spread the false message (just like he used Eve to spread the lie to Adam and eventually to billions). Some influential men spread the idea to others and it spread until even some bible scholars began to fall for it and now many believe the cover up.

It shouldn't be hard to believe that the fallen angels do not want you to know about some of the evil that angels have done and the evil they are currently doing as you read this book...and the evil they plan to do to the human race. While the fallen angels are infinitely inferior to God and infinitely less knowledgeable than God, they are far more powerful than humans and far more knowledgeable than humans. That's why Satan was able to easily deceive Adam and Eve...and why he has easily deceived billions of humans (even today). And why the biggest deception ever is coming soon.

Matthew 24:24
24 For false christs and false prophets will arise and perform **great signs and wonders**, so as to lead astray, if possible, even the elect. (ESV)

2 Thessalonians 2:11
9 The coming of the lawless one is by the activity of Satan with all power and **false signs and wonders**, **10** and with all **wicked deception** for those who are perishing, because they refused to love the truth and so be saved. **11** Therefore God sends them **a strong delusion**, so that they may believe what is **false**. (ESV)

Ephesians 6:12
12 For we do not wrestle against **flesh and blood**, but against the rulers, against the authorities, against the cosmic powers over this present darkness, against the **spiritual** forces of evil in the **heavenly places**. (ESV)

Jesus Christ defeated Satan at the cross and our God will surely prevail again in the final war that will take place at a location called Armageddon...but we must open our eyes because the deception is far deeper than we originally thought.

Hang tight, I'll soon show you where the Bible tells us the name and current location of the 666-beast (i.e. the antichrist). But without clearing up some of this background information, it is hard to understand that portion of the Bible. It would be like skipping basic math and going straight into college calculus.

Chapter 7

☼ **Can Angels Get Married?**

The more details we know about that time period which is covered in the Bible, the clearer the Bible becomes and the easier it is to connect the dots. For example, is it true that angels had sex with humans? This point is critical to our understanding of the beasts in Revelation. It is especially helpful to know more about the nature of the second beast. This crime committed by the fallen elohim is the main issue behind most of the entire Bible. Mating with humans to create hybrid Nephilim is probably the biggest chess move that Satan and his faction of angels made in the Bible epic. The fact that rogue elohim had sexual intercourse to get the human females pregnant, and thereby tainting the original human DNA, explains many things that would otherwise remain unclear. That forbidden sex explains the great flood of Noah, it explains the numerous battles such as David and Goliath. It also explains why God commanded his Israelites to kill Children, widows and breast feeding infants. I don't see how anyone can follow the story line in the Bible without first understanding that fallen elohim created a new bloodline, the bloodline of the Nephilim. There are different beliefs and interpretations about Genesis 6:1-4, which leaves many Christians feeling like this sex topic might remain unsettled and debatable until the lord Jesus Christ returns and Christians can ask him face to face. It might remain debatable for many Christians, however, the reader of this book will probably learn the answer and become confident that they've found the truth right in the Bible. My goal is not to simply tell you the answer but it's to show you where the answer is in the Bible. The main points addressed in this book are supported by careful study and analysis of the actual Holy Bible (the ancient scrolls and codices that the English translations are taken from, plus new findings like the Dead Sea Scrolls). Here is a Bible quote that is often central in the discussion of this topic.

Genesis 6:1-4
And it came to pass, when men began to multiply on the face of the earth, and daughters were born unto them, ² That the sons of God saw the daughters of men that they *were* fair; and they took them wives of all which they chose. ³ And the LORD said, My spirit shall not always strive with man, for that he also *is* flesh: yet his days shall be an hundred and twenty years. ⁴ There were giants in the earth in those days; and also after that, when the sons of God came in unto the daughters of men, and they bare *children* to them, the same *became* mighty men which *were* of old, men of renown. (King James Version, "KJV")

In the English translations, the above four verses provide almost enough biblical evidence to prove to Christians that Angels had sex with humans. While it is almost enough in the English translations, it is definitely enough in the ancient Hebrew manuscripts of the Bible. This point is explained more thoroughly in later chapters. For now, however, keep in mind that the English translations are "ATTEMPTED" translations of something that cannot be perfectly translated into English. That is why there are dozens of English Bible versions.

Why does the topic of this book seem to be debatable and unsettled? There is only one story in the entire Bible that people can point to when they try to make the argument that it could not have been angles that "came into the daughters of men" in Gen 6:4. They say Genesis 6:1-4 could not possibly be talking about angels because the New Testament says that

80

angels are physically incapable of having sexual intercourse. The opponents of this book say that the bodies of angels lack the required anatomy to have sex with a human so it's impossible. But where in the bible does it say that? It actually does not say that in the Bible and this book will prove it. That portion of the Bible will be parsed (analyzed and broken down) for the reader so that the point of this book becomes obvious. It is erroneous to point to this Gospel story in the bible in an effort to prove that (due to the anatomy of angels) they are physically incapable of having sex.

As you probably know, many of the Gospel stories are retold in two or more of the four New Testament gospels. The story about "angels" not marrying appears in three out of the four Gospels. An important technique used in analyzing pivotal verses in the Bible is to read them slowly paying close attention to each word. This story is where the apostles are asking Jesus about a woman that got married and her first husband died. So she was required to marry the brother of her deceased husband. Her first husband died so she married one of his brothers. There were seven brothers and each new husband died so she ended up marrying all seven of them. The idea of marrying the brother of the deceased is known as the levirate marriage in Israelite tradition (Deuteronomy 25:5-6). So the Apostles asked Jesus, in the resurrection, whose wife of the seven will she be. Here is their question as translated into English in the Gospel of Matthew.

Matthew 22:25-28
Now there were with us seven brethren: and the first, when he had married a wife, deceased, and, having no [children], left his wife unto his brother: 26 Likewise the second also, and the third, unto the seventh. 27 And

last of all the woman died also. [28] Therefore in the resurrection whose wife shall she be of the seven? for they all had her. (KJV)

The response that Jesus himself gave to the above question is recounted in three of the four gospels. The words of Jesus are seen in the following verses and are printed in red in some Bibles (in the translations that use red to indicate the words spoken by Jesus).

Matthew 22:29-30
Jesus answered and said unto them, Ye do err, not knowing the scriptures, nor the power of God. [30] For in the resurrection they neither marry, nor are given in marriage, but are as the angels of God in heaven. (KJV)

Mark 12:24-25
And Jesus answering said unto them, Do ye not therefore err, because ye know not the scriptures, neither the power of God? [25] For when they shall rise from the dead, they neither marry, nor are given in marriage; but are as the angels which are in heaven. (KJV)

Luke 20:34-36
And Jesus answering said unto them, The children of this world marry, and are given in marriage: [35] But they which shall be accounted worthy to obtain that world, and the resurrection from the dead, neither marry, nor are given in marriage: [36] Neither can they die any more: for they are equal unto the angels; and are the children of God, being the children of the resurrection. (KJV)

All three Gospels clearly state that the humans will neither marry nor be given in marriage. Who is it that will neither marry nor be given in marriage? ...the resurrected HUMANS, not the angels. All three gospels are clear that what Jesus is saying about marriage applies in the RESURRECTION, not here on Earth. Both Matthew and Mark include the words "in heaven" while Luke says "that world", instead of "in heaven". What world was Jesus talking about in Luke when he said "that world". Instead of "that world", some translations say "that age" in Luke 20:35. Remember that there is a new heaven and a new earth after the resurrection (see Revelation 21:1 and Isaiah 65:17). Jesus wanted to clarify that this marriage situation applies in the new heaven and the new earth to come. Obviously, it does not apply here on this earth.

Furthermore, the Gospel of Matthew says that the resurrected humans will be like the ANGELS OF GOD IN HEAVEN. The Angels of who? Jesus is talking about God's angels not Satan's angels. The angels of God where? Jesus said in heaven, not on Earth. What about Satan's angels on earth? Matthew is clear that Jesus was talking about the angels of God in Heaven. Why did God want Matthew to include in his Holy Scriptures the words "Angels of God in Heaven". Do you think that maybe it's just a filler to waste papyrus and ink for no reason? No. Did God simply want to use a certain writing style for artistic reasons? No. And what about Mark? Why does Mark say "Angels in Heaven"? Does Mark also like to waste papyrus? No. Are there really some throw away words in the Bible? No. Christians should not be so quick to regard some of the words in the Bible as fillers or unimportant throw-away words. As seen in Matthew 5:18, each and every letter of God's word is important.

Matthew 5:18
For truly I say to you until heaven and earth pass away not an iota not a dot will pass from the Law until all is accomplished. (ESV)

Matthew 5:18
For verily I say unto you, Till heaven and earth pass, one jot or one tittle shall in no wise pass from the law, till all be fulfilled. (KJV)

Matthew adds the following words to again show how important the word of God is.

Matthew 24:35
Heaven and earth shall pass away, but my words shall not pass away. (KJV)

Going back to Luke chapter 20, there is some clarifying detail about what Jesus said with regards to Angels. Here is the verse.

Luke 20:34-36
And Jesus answering said unto them, The children of <u>this</u> world marry, and are given in marriage: ³⁵ But <u>they</u> which shall be accounted worthy to obtain that world, and the resurrection from the dead, neither marry, nor are given in marriage: ³⁶ Neither can they <u>die</u> any more: for they are equal unto the angels; and are the children of God, being the children of the <u>resurrection</u>. (KJV)

The underlined portions in the above verse would be in red colored text in some Bibles to show that those are the words of Jesus himself. Jesus said that the reason resurrected humans cannot <u>die</u> anymore is because they are equal to angels and are children of God. It doesn't say that the reason humans cannot have <u>SEX</u> anymore is because they are equal to angels. Humans cannot <u>DIE</u> because they are equal to angels. In other words, resurrected humans do not marry in the resurrection, period. And since humans become equal to angels, they cannot die anymore. The author of this book realizes that the English translations seem to imply that the angels of God in Heaven do not get married. However, it does not say that. Luke adds the missing detail when he wrote that resurrected humans cannot <u>die</u> anymore because humans become like angels and are "children of God" due to being children of the resurrection.

So which Gospel quoted Jesus more accurately? Matthew, Mark or Luke? Before answering that, lets look at another story in the Gospels that sheds light on how the Gospels were written. One of the stories about Jesus healing the blind is told in three of the Gospels (Mark 10:46, Matthew 20:30 and Luke 18:35). Mark and Matthew talk about one blind man being healed while Luke talks about two blind men being healed. Was it one or was it two? Is there a contradiction in the Bible? There is no contradiction here. It's just that Luke provides additional detail. If Nancy says that Ronald has a daughter but later you find out that he has a son and a daughter, would you think that Nancy lied? No, maybe Nancy only mentioned the daughter because Nancy is the schoolteacher of Ronald's daughter. Also, Luke says that Jesus healed the blind men while Jesus was approaching Jericho while Mark and Matthew say that the healing took place while Jesus was on his way out of Jericho. How can that contradiction be reconciled? Do not worry, you can breathe easy about this because you will find that there are two cities that were called Jericho in the first century. There was the Jericho of the Old Testament, which in the first century was just a tiny village by the old ruins of the Old Testament Jericho. Then there was the newer Jericho built by Herod the King located about two miles Southwest of the old one.

So think back to the question of which Gospel was more accurate about the lack of marriage in the resurrection. All three are accurate but Luke adds some detail. Luke clarifies it by adding that Jesus said that resurrected humans cannot die and that is what makes them like the angels of God. It is not the lack of marriage that makes resurrected humans equal to angels. Rather it is the immortal nature that makes resurrected humans equal to angels. Even if Christians still want to believe that it is indeed the lack of marriage that will make humans like angels, it is still a stretch to assume that it is the lack of required sex anatomy that will make humans equal to angels. It may or may not be that something similar to sex but better than sex will exist in heaven? And what if in heaven there is no need for marriage. Even if the required anatomy for sex is missing from humans and angels in heaven, the Bible does not say that angels cannot gain that ability when they are here on Earth. Do angels need to eat human food when they are in heaven? When they step out of the supernatural realm and materialize into flesh and blood form, angels can eat human food as seen in Genesis 19:3. The angels of God in heaven do not have sex but the angels of Satan on Earth were capable. The fact that Satan's angels had sex here on earth will be proven later in this book by clear undisputable Bible verses.

Even if Jesus did mean to imply that "angels of God in Heaven" do not get married then he certainly did qualify it by clearly stating that it applies to "angels of God in Heaven" rather than saying that it applies to all angels. If it applied to all angels including the fallen angels of Satan, then why did he say "...angels of God in Heaven..." in Matthew and why did he say in Mark "...like angels in heaven...". Jesus could have simply said that resurrected humans are like angels period. Jesus doesn't tell us what it is that angels do when they leave heaven to get out of the kingdom of God and thereby become fallen angels. The disobedient angels are not "angels of God in Heaven". And the fact that angels did leave their heavenly body is shown in Jude 6. Later in this book, the Greek word *oiketerion* (in Jude 6) is shown to be the heavenly body that the souls of angels occupy just like the soul of a human occupies a temporary flesh and blood body. It seems that the human body (the perishable tent) may be a type of "oiketerion".

Although Jesus is quoted in three different Gospels about marriage in heaven, none of those Gospels say that angels physically cannot have sex due to their anatomy. Furthermore, the context is about the angels of God in heaven not the angels of Satan on Earth. Those are two very different groups of angels. This is not an opinion, it is a fact of your bible. So even if you believe that Jesus is talking about whether or not angels of God in Heaven can get married, the Bible certainly does not say that they are physically incapable of sexual intercourse. Instead it says that they do not get married when they are in heaven. There is very big difference between not doing something and being physically incapable of doing it. When bank tellers are in the bank working, they do not run around naked in front of customers. That is what bank tellers do not do when they are in the bank working. To say that bank tellers do not do that in the bank is not the same as saying that they are physically incapable of running around naked. So why assume that the tellers are physically incapable of running around naked when they are at home. Maybe bank tellers run around naked at home or at a nude community.

Each Gospel writer might use different words for the same story. It does not mean he only healed one blind man, or two or forty. It just means that one of the Gospels writers wrote

87

about one of the blind men while the other wrote about two of the blind men. Since this difference in the Gospels is common, it should be a clear sign that none of the Gospels said that the issue was the lack of required anatomy for sex. The Bible had three opportunities for three different Gospel writers to write the words physically cannot, or physically impossible, or due to incapable anatomy or something to make it clear. But none of the three Gospel writers wrote anything like that. The question of angels having sex with humans makes such an enormous difference in how one understands the Bible that it would make sense for God to have made it clear if sex was impossible for angels. Or perhaps God wanted it to be revealed at the right time. Instead of God using one of the three Gospel opportunities to say that it is impossible, God made it clear in the ancient manuscripts so that when it became more important for Christians to know this, it could be known. Now that we are so much closer to the return of Christ, it is becoming increasingly important to understand that angels did have sex with humans and why it matters.

Jesus was not saying what the angels do or do not do when they are out of Heaven and out of God's kingdom. He's not addressing what they do or do not do when they are on earth. Angels do far more atrocious things than just have sex with humans, far more atrocious. Every atrocity in human history every bad thing that has happened in human history can be tied back to these fallen angels, everything. And that is a whole different book.

In the Bible, does the word "marriage" (or other forms of the word "marry") have the same definition as the word "sex" (or "fornicate")? We know that the answer is no because Jesus

Christ will marry the Christian Church. Look at the word "marriage" in Revelation 19:7-9. The "marriage" of Jesus Christ and the Church is called a big mystery in Ephesians 5:32. Furthermore, there are other words that are used in the Bible that mean sex or intercourse. Jesus did not haphazardly speak his words when he was answering the apostles about which of the seven brothers will she belong to. Jesus was never careless about his choice of words. And neither did the Gospel writers carelessly quote Jesus. All three Gospel writers had the chance to use a word that meant sex or intercourse. All three had the chance to be clear if it was an issue of physical anatomy.

One thing is clear and undisputable; Jesus did not clearly say that it is physically impossible for all angels to have sex. Therefore, a set of assumptions would be required to believe that Jesus implied that. In order to believe that angels lack the anatomy to have sex and to believe that it is physically impossible for any and all angels to have sex, one must make ALL of the following assumptions;

1. When Jesus said marriage he also meant sexual intercourse.
2. When Jesus said that resurrected humans "are as angels" or "equal to angels" he meant that the physical anatomy of angels is the same as the new imperishable body of resurrected Christians.
3. When Jesus said "angels of God in Heaven" in Matthew or "angels which are in heaven" in Mark, he was also including the fallen angels of Satan. This assumption deals with whether the angels in question are God's angels or Satan's angels.

4. When Jesus said "in Heaven" in the book of Matthew or "in heaven" in the book of Mark, he was also including the fallen angels located on Earth (i.e. not just in Heaven). This assumption deals with the location of the angels.

Some Christians might continue to make those assumptions after reading this book. At least now, however, they can be aware of the fact that they are making a series of assumptions in order to get the Bible to fit within their pre-existing belief system. This might be a tough pill to swallow for some. It was certainly a tough pill for me to swallow.

Some parts of this book make a distinction between the actual Bible and the attempted translations into English. Most Bible scholars consider the Biblica Hebraica Stuttgartensia ("BHS") to be the most authoritative and accurate compilation of the Old Testament. The BHS is a complete collection of the textual tradition of the Hebrew Bible which was compiled by Jewish rabbis. These particular Jewish rabbis which dedicated their life to preserving and restoring the original writings were called Masoretes. The BHS[3] is considered by many Bible scholars to be the authoritative Hebrew text and is used by most Bible versions as the core foundation from which to base their interpretations. However, some Jewish rabbis rebuke the BHS because it is produced by the Germans who tried to exterminate the Jews in the Jewish holocaust. Furthermore, there is a scribal error[4] in the Masoretic text (a

---

[3] The BHS is not the only source used by the various English translations. Most English translations use more than one source such as the Latin Vulgate or the Septuagint. After 1991, the modern day translations have a huge advantage now that the Dead Sea Scrolls have been released to the general public.
[4] There is more than one scribal error but only one of those is significant to the main topic of this book.

typo) that is discussed later in this book. In addition to the Masoretic texts, some translations supplement their translation work with the Dead Sea Scrolls and other ancient writings (e.g. Septuagint and the Samaritan Pentateuch) which provide some clarification of certain passages.

Chapter 8

Greek Grammar For Jude

The question of whether or not Angels had sexual intercourse with humans is clearly answered if you study the entire Bible. That topic is not so clear if you look at only one verse or only one chapter. There is one book in the Bible, however, that makes it perfectly clear in a single page. The book of Jude. However, that perfect clarity is only evident in the ancient Greek manuscripts because the Greek grammar rules make it easier to follow the writing in Jude. The good news is that you don't have to become an expert in Greek grammar to see such level of clarity with your own eyes. There are two verses that make this clear in the bible. One is in the Old Testament and one in the New Testament. And then there are several other verses that support it and further clarify it.

Most of you know the Genesis 6:2 verse which is the verse that reveals to us in good detail what had happened. Angels (more accurately, "elohim") actually married the daughters of the humans and (as a result) the human females birthed giants. The women birthed these nephilims for these angels (more accurately these fallen elohim). So most of you are familiar with that verse. However, not all Christians are familiar with the fact that Jude 7 is even clearer. Jude actually comes right out and tells us plainly that angels had sexual intercourse with human females. But Jude 7 is a verse that is difficult to translate into English. Only one English translation that I am aware of actually translated it in a way such that it gets the accurate message across more definitively. The other translations do say it. However they say it in such a way that people could read it more than one way. Not that it was written to mean more than one thing because the actual Bible is not at all ambiguous. The Greek text doesn't have two different ways that you could read it but when you translate it to English you suddenly end up with two possible ways you could read it. Jude 7 says that Sodom and Gomorrah **AND** the cities around them (i.e. that whole group of cities) committed the sin of forbidden sex and equates it to the same exact sin that was committed by the angels. The Greek grammar rules let those that read it in Greek know to group together Sodom and Gomorrah plus the cities around Sodom and Gomorrah and to make that entire group of cities the subject. That one group of **CITIES** committed the same exact identical sin that the angles did, of sexually immorality (i.e. going after strange flesh). It just means they went after flesh that was not of their own kind (or having sex with flesh that was unnatural for them). The Angels didn't have sex with angels. The Angels were having sex with humans. That part becomes evident in Genesis 6:2. (Note: after the resurrection, Jesus had a different kind of body than the one he had before he was crucified).

So where do I get this idea that Jude 7 is even more clear than Genesis 6:2. Well, we have to take a look at the Greek writings and the Greek grammar rules. If you follow the Greek grammar rules you cannot understand it more than one way you can only see it one way. And yes, I do believe that with some verses in the Bible, God intended to give us more than one meaning because a passage might apply to the spiritual realm in one sense while the same passage had a similar but different meaning in the worldly realm. But when a bible verse has more than one meaning, both meanings are in harmony with each other. In other words, if you find a verse that seems to have two meanings but one meaning is contradictory to the other, then something is wrong. In that case, the contradiction only exists in the English translations. So you'll have to do some research to get to the bottom of it but it's beautiful when you do see the original ancient meaning because it's in harmony. In other words, this whole idea (that is ramped among American Christian congregations today) that "it depends on how you interpret it" is a lie from Satan spreading like a virus infecting the American Christian congregations. Listen, IT DOES NOT DEPEND ON HOW YOU INTERPRET THAT VERSE (i.e. and I mean any verse in the Bible). There is only one way to interpret the ancient writings. In English, yes, you might get a whole set of different possible ways to interpret a verse. But not in the actual Bible. Satan wants you to think that there is more than one way to interpret a verse. Satan is very smart. If Satan can convince the American Church of that lie then the entire Bible is much more elastic and then God's original meaning is bendable now. How far can you bend it? In what direction can you bend it? It is a lie from the pits of hell and most of the American Church has bought it hook line and sinker. If it seems to the reader of the Bible that a verse could have two or more interpretations and both interpretations are not in perfect harmony, then it simply means that the original ancient Bible is not translatable into English in that verse.

The issue with the Greek manuscript for Jude is that there are grammar rules that exist in the biblical Greek that don't exist in the English language. For example, in English, you could say "the boy kicked the pony". In that English sentence, how do we know who kicked who? In that sentence we know that the boy was the one that kicked the pony. We don't read that and wonder if maybe it was the pony that kicked the boy. We know that it wasn't the pony that did the kicking. It was the boy that did the kicking because of the English grammar rules. As you read English, you might not be thinking about the grammar because a lot of the English grammar rules just come naturally to you because you were learning to speak since you were a tiny little child. And at the time, you didn't even know the definition of the word "grammar". So they were just engrained in you so you don't think anything of it when somebody says the boy kicked the pony you're not sitting there thinking "Hum lets see, what are the rules so I can figure out who kicked who"…no, it just comes naturally from years of hearing others talk and doing your own talking. So, you might not have ever thought that maybe other languages have different grammar rules. In English the reason you know it's the boy that did the kicking is because the boy came first in the sentence prior to the verb so the subject is the one that comes first in that sentence structure and the subject comes before the verb therefore the subject performs the verb onto the object which is the pony. So those are some English grammar rules. If you wanted to say that the kicker was not the boy and that instead it was the pony that kicked the boy, all you have to do is switch the words around. Put pony before the word kicked and put the word boy after the verb (kicking) and now the pony kicked the boy. Now you know that it was the pony doing the kicking. Well in Greek there is no such grammar rule. In first century Biblical Koine Greek, it doesn't matter if you put the word boy before the word kick or after. It doesn't matter. You could switch the pony and boy all day long it wouldn't make any difference. The reader of the Greek knows exactly who did the kicking not by where the subject is placed relative to the verb in the sentence, or to the object, but by an entirely different grammatical convention. Why, because there are special letters attached to the subject and to the object so wherever you place the word in the sentence that special letter goes with it to let the reader know if that word is the subject or the object.

> (Note: in Greek, these are known as "cases. Type the following 3 words as a sentence into an internet search engine ["Greek cases explained"] and study about the nominative case and the accusative case as well as the "nominative-accusative")

And those special letters denote whether or not that word is in the nominative case or accusative case or one of the other cases. If a noun is in the nominative case then it is the one performing the action of the verb to the noun that is in the accusative case. In other words, the noun in the nominative case is dealing out the kick and the noun in the accusative case is receiving the kick (Note: kicking is the verb in this example).

For Jude 6-7, Dr. Kenneth Wuest (a leader on the team of interpreters of the New American Standard Bible) provides the following insight. This is an excerpt from his book entitled;

"Wuest's Word Studies in the Greek New Testament"
by Kenneth S. Wuest

This verse [Jude 7] begins with *hos* (ὅς), an adverb of comparison having the meanings of "in the same manner as, after the fashion of, as, just as." Here it introduces a comparison showing a likeness between the angels of verse 6 and the cities of Sodom and Gomorrha of this verse. But the likeness between them lies deeper than the fact that both were guilty of committing sin. It extends to the fact that both were guilty of the same identical sin. The punctuation of the Authorized Version ("AV") is misleading, as an examination of Greek text discloses.

The A.V. punctuation gives the reader the impression that Sodom and Gomorrha committed fornication and that the cities about them committed fornication in like manner to the two cities named. The phrase "in like manner" is according to the punctuation construed with the words "the cities about them." A rule of Greek grammar comes into play here. The word "cities" is in the nominative case. The words "in like manner" are in the accusative case and are classified as an adverbial accusative by Dana and Mantey in their *Manual Grammar of the Greek New Testament* (pp. 91, 93). This latter construction is related syntactically, not with a word in the nominative case but with the verbal form in the sentence. All of which means that the words "in like manner" are related to the verbal forms, "giving themselves over to fornication" and "going after strange flesh." In addition to all this, the Greek text has *toutois* (τουτοις), "to these." Thus, the translation should read, "just as Sodom and Gomorrha and the cities about them, in like manner to these, having given themselves over to fornication and having gone after strange flesh." The sense of the entire passage (vv. 6, 7) is that the cities of Sodom and Gomorrha and the cities about them, in like manner to these (the angels), have given themselves over to fornication and have gone after strange flesh. That means that the sin of the fallen angels was fornication. This sin on the part of the angels is described in the words, "going after strange flesh." The word "strange" is *heteros* (ἑτερος), "another of a different kind." That is, these angels transgressed the limits of their own natures to invade a realm of created beings of a different nature. This invasion took the form of fornication, a cohabitation with beings of a different nature from theirs. This takes us back to Genesis 6:1–4 where we have the account of the sons of God (here, fallen angels), cohabiting with women of the human race. For a discussion of this subject, the reader is referred to the author's volumes [i.e. Wuest's volumes], *First Peter in the Greek New Testament* (pp. 97–107), and *The Practical use of the Greek New Testament* (pp.31–35).

The words describing both the sin of the angels and of the inhabitants of Sodom and Gomorrha, "giving themselves over to fornication" are the translation of *ekporneuō* (ἐκπορνευω). The prefixed preposition *ek* (ἐκ) indicates in the usage of the word a lust that gluts itself, satisfies itself completely. The force of *ek* (ἐκ) which itself means "out," is "out and out." It signifies a giving of one's self utterly. The words "strange flesh," that is, flesh of a different and in this case an opposite (diametrically opposed) nature, speak of the angels' intercourse with women, the latter being forbidden flesh. The sin of the angels was against nature. In the case of the cities mentioned, it was the sin which Paul mentions in Romans 1:27, a departure from the natural use and against nature.

[This marks the end of the quoted excerpt from Kenneth S Wuest]

The Greek grammar rules make it clear to the reader of the Greek that ALL the cities around Sodom and Gomorrah (including Sodom and Gomorrah) were all guilty of the same identical sin that the angels committed of sexual intercourse with a type of flesh that they were not supposed to be having sex with, period. A Bible scholar cannot possibly claim that he gains a better understanding of Jude by reading the English translations than the understanding he would gain from direct examination of the ancient Greek manuscripts.

Also, verse numbers and chapter numbers were added by humans centuries after the Autographs were written. The location of the verse numbers causes problems when reading the Bible. The location of the verse numbers creates a division and a sense of separation which influences the readers understanding as they read. Notice how different the Bible is when you listen to the Bible through an audio book. An audio Bible is a great addition to your study tools. Those verse numbers were not in the original word of God so they are not in a sacred position. Don't let the verse numbers influence your reading because it might lead you to some erroneous conclusions. To piece together the puzzle of the 666-beast, one must gain a more complete picture of the spiritual realm. A Bible reader that lacks a clear understanding that the Son's of God in Genesis 6:1-4 are supernatural beings that existed before this planet was created is going to struggle with this topic of the 666-beast because the supernatural realm is still too unclear for them. If you're still not sure of the identity of the Son's of God in Genesis 6, then I strongly recommend that you read major works and commentaries from both sides of the debate. Do not simply read the ones that already support your disbelief that elohim had sex with humans (carefully read BOTH).

Chapter 9

☼ **Bible or Attempted Translation**

As mentioned earlier in this book, there are no chapters or verses in the actual Bible. There was no indication of when a sentence ended or a paragraph ended or when a story ended or when a chapter begins. None of that. You just read continuously. It was like somebody was just talking to you. When they talk to you they don't say ok that was the end of that chapter and here's the beginning of the next chapter. They just keep talking and each book of the bible is like one conversation. Without paragraphs without periods and that's just one of the many things that make the Bible untranslatable into English. It is actually not something that can be translated into English. There are over thirty attempted translations into the English language.

The following list includes some of the attempts to translate the actual Bible manuscripts into English;

1. English Standard Version
2. New American Standard Bible
3. The Good News Translation
4. New International Version
5. 1890 Darby Bible
6. American Standard Version
7. King James Version (a.k.a. The Authorized Version)
8. The Contemporary English Version
9. God's Word
10. New International Version

11. The Holman Christian Standard Bible
12. Newberry Interlinear Literal Translation of The Greek New Testament
13. International Standard Version
14. Jewish New Testament
15. The Living Bible, Paraphrased
16. Luther Bibel
17. The Message
18. Nestle-Aland Greek New Testament, 27th Edition
19. The New American Bible
20. The New Century Version
21. The New Jerusalem Bible
22. The New King James Version
23. The New Living Translation
24. The Revised Standard Version
25. The New Revised Standard Version
26. Young's Literal Translation
27. Wescott-Hort Greek New Testament
28. Amplified Bible
29. Wycliffe Bible
30. World English
31. Weymouth New Testament
32. Tyndale New Testament
33. Jubilee Bible 2000

All Bible's in the English language should be viewed as ATTEMPTED translations and NOT as the actual Bible itself. Because the actual Bible cannot be entirely translated into English and you will see why. But don't be concerned or afraid because most English translations are very good attempts and a lot of the true message does get across. Most of the important theological points are still conveyed well enough to ensure our eternal salvation. If you asked me for a recommendation on

Bible translations, I would say the top two in the list above. Better than that, however, would be parallel Bible reading. A good parallel Bible tool that I use a lot is www.biblehub.com (I have no affiliation with biblehub.com). There is software that allows you to read a verse in several translations side by side. Reading the Bible in this parallel approach is an extremely powerful way to study the Bible. We should be honest with ourselves that we are at a disadvantage and that we are missing much of the richness and critical details contained in the actual Bible. We are blessed that Jesus Christ went to send us the Holy Spirit of God who helps us to grow our understanding of the scriptures. But let's not lose sight of the fact that we are in a struggle and it is not against flesh and blood humans (Ephesians 6:12). You have to ask yourself this question… "am I qualified to determine which of the thirty plus translations is most accurate?". None of them are 100 percent accurate. Never will there be an English translation that gives the reader the full meaning and richness of the manuscripts.

Throughout this book, the word autograph may be used instead of the word manuscript. Manuscripts are extremely reliable and amazingly accurate handmade copies of the original autograph. The difference is that the word "autograph" refers to the very first writing of that book, which contained the original ink and original medium written by the original author himself. In other words, a manuscript is a copy while an "autograph" is the original.

The ancient Biblical languages are far too different than the English language. Furthermore, the era in which the original autographs were written was so different with regards to the culture and social norms that many critically important words cannot be fully understood without a thorough understanding of the ancient culture that existed when the autographs were written. There are words in the manuscripts that don't exist in the English language. So what do we do? To really define that word it requires like sometimes an entire paragraph unto itself. When translators attempt to translate the actual Bible into English, they can't take one of the words and replace that one word with a whole paragraph. So the translators have no choice but to put words in there that might be close to the original meaning. Unfortunately, there is nothing even close in some cases. Check out the mechanical translation at [www.mechanical-translation.org] and also at [www.ancient-hebrew.org]. You can see in those webpages part of the reason why it's not possible to make an accurate translation into English.

In ancient Biblical Hebrew, each letter has a meaning all on its own. So each ancient Hebrew letter is like a word or even a sentence. Each letter is a picture of a tangible object that any civilization in any era can grasp. For example, the first ancient Hebrew letter was a picture of the head of an Ox or Bull (similar to American Indian petroglyphs or ancient Egyptian hieroglyphs). The ancient Hebrew letter for N is called Nun and it's a picture of a seed sprouting. The second letter B is called Bet and it's a picture of a house. So if you put those two ancient Hebrew letters together you get BN which means "sprouts from the house of" or descendant of that house. The Bet letter could also mean the family in that house or the house of that family. The N tells you that it's a seed sprouting or a new shoot from a tree. It would never mean a non-blood relative and it would always mean in the bloodline and more frequently direct bloodline (i.e. son, grandson, great grandson, and so forth). Because you would not have an apple seedling that sprouted from the seed of an orange. Some letters can even require several English words just to define that one single letter. So imagine if you have a three letter word or a six letter word, you've got not one word you've got six letters which are six words and sometimes it take two or three words to define just one of the letters. So when you pile on the various challenges that translators run into, you can see why none of the English translations are 100% accurate...none ever will be.

So one Hebrew word could require a whole paragraph to properly express the nuanced meaning of that word since it doesn't exist in the English language. If each ancient Hebrew letter of each ancient Hebrew word was accurately explained, the bible might be seven times thicker than it is. And what about English grammar rules. The attempted English translations would be even more unreadable if the translators included words to let the reader know whether a Greek word is in the accusative case or in the nominative case or one of the other Greek cases. I suppose it might take two or three whole books to adequately demonstrate that the bible cannot be accurately translated into English. ALL Bibles in the English language are just attempted translations and so we're missing a lot of detail. The translation problems are just one of the reasons why the topic of this book (i.e. the 666-Beast) has been so easy for the enemy of Jesus to hide from the main stream American congregations.

Chapter 10

☿ **Angels Materialize Into Human Form**

The fact that angels have this ability to step out of the invisible realm and materialize into the realm that is visible to humans is evident in the Bible. And that their physical flesh and blood body that they materialize into is capable of performing human bodily function. And the fact that they did leave their heavenly body is shown in Jude 6 through a study of the word (οἰκητήριον [*oiketerion* /oy·kay·tay·ree·on/]). In Jude 6, two different words are used to express that they left two different places and abandoned two different things (not just one thing).

Jude 6

And angels who had not kept their own original <u>state</u>, but had abandoned their own <u>dwelling</u>, he keeps in eternal chains under gloomy darkness, to the judgment of the great day; (the Darby English translation)

Angels left both their original <u>STATE</u> AND their own <u>DWELLING</u>. That's two separate words with two separate meanings in the Greek. The word State refers to their general habitat (i.e their realm or something akin to the term geographic location) while the word Dwelling refers to the body of their soul/spirit which is probably much like the new body that we humans will get when we go to the new heaven and the new earth. Just like human souls/spirits dwell in this temporary flesh and blood body).

107

An angel is capable of serving food to a human.

1 Kings 19:5-8
5 And he lay down and slept under a broom tree. And behold, an **angel** touched him and said to him, "**Arise and eat**." **6** And he looked, and behold, there was at his head a cake **baked on hot stones** and a jar of water. And he ate and drank and lay down again. **7** And the **angel of the Lord** came again a second time and touched him and said, "**Arise and eat**, for the journey is too great for you." **8** And he arose and ate and drank, and went in the strength of **that food** forty days and forty nights to Horeb, the mount of God. (ESV)

Where did that angel get the cake and the jar of water? I don't know but it seems "The Angel of The Lord" baked the cake on hot stones. And when you think about it, you realize that there's so much about angels that we don't know. That's important because it makes us think carefully about verses instead of speeding past important words in the Bible. These important words help to give us a clearer picture since we can now see more pieces of the puzzle. The more pieces of the puzzle that we have in place, the more likely it is that we'll understand the next piece we find and where that next piece fits. They physically performed a physical action that requires a physical body to perform, which is making or acquiring food for a human (whether supernaturally or in a more human like manner). They also had food cooked for them and they ate it.

Genesis 19:1-3
The two angels came to Sodom in the evening, and Lot was sitting in the gate of Sodom. When Lot saw them, he rose to meet them and bowed himself with his face to the earth **2** and said, "My lords, please turn aside to your servant's house and spend the night and wash your feet. Then you may rise up early and go on your way." They said, "No; we will spend the night in the

town square." ³ But he pressed them strongly; so they turned aside to him and entered his house. And he made them a feast and baked unleavened bread, and they ate. (ESV)

And that's not the only time that angels ate food cooked by humans.

Genesis 18:1-8
And the L**ORD** appeared to him by the oaks of Mamre, as he sat at the door of his tent in the heat of the day. ² He lifted up his eyes and looked, and behold, **three men** were standing in front of him. When he saw them, he ran from the tent door to meet them and bowed himself to the earth ³ and said, "O **Lord**, if I have found favor in your sight, do not pass by your servant. ⁴ Let a little water be brought, and wash your feet, and rest yourselves under the tree, ⁵ while I bring a morsel of bread, that you may refresh yourselves, and after that you may pass on—since you have come to your servant." So they said, "**Do as you have said**." ⁶ And Abraham went quickly into the tent to Sarah and said, "Quick! Three seahs of fine flour! Knead it, and make cakes." ⁷ And Abraham ran to the herd and took a calf, tender and good, and gave it to a young man, who prepared it quickly. ⁸ Then he took curds and milk and the calf that he had prepared, and set it before them. And he stood by them under the tree while they ate. (ESV)

Did you notice that one of the men in that gathering was referred to as "the Lord"? Verse 1 says "And the Lord". Abraham ran to the 3 "men" and said "O Lord" to one of the 3 "men". The reason they are called "men" is because angels can look just like humans. One of those 3 men was possibly the elohim that later manifested into Jesus Christ of Nazareth. Jesus existed long before this planet was created (see John 1:1-5).

Hebrews 13:2

² Do not neglect to show hospitality to strangers, for thereby some have entertained angels <u>unawares</u>. (ESV)

Hebrews 13:2 tells us that it has happened to some people that they were interacting with what they thought was just a human stranger but it was actually an angel. That's why angels are called "men" in some parts of the Bible.

Daniel 9:21

²¹ while I was speaking in prayer, the man Gabriel, whom I had seen in the vision at the first, came to me in <u>swift flight</u> at the time of the evening sacrifice. (ESV)

It is obvious in the book of Daniel that Gabriel is an angel. Humans were not arriving in "swift flight" at the time that the book of Daniel was written. Yet this angel called Gabriel, was called "the **man** Gabriel". By the way, if some English translations refer to the beasts of Revelation as "man", it doesn't mean that such a beast is human in the same way the Gabriel is not human. I mention this here because some people say that the 666-beast will be a human yet nothing in the Bible indicates that the 666-beast will be human. In fact, all indications are clear that the 666-beast will NOT be human.

When you look back at Genesis chapter 18, those angels were eating with Abraham. Eating is a flesh and blood bodily function. They also had their feet washed. Elohim (some are angels) can step out of the invisible spiritual realm and into the visible human realm and disappear again into the invisible realm. There are instances in the Bible where angels suddenly became invisible while humans looked on to witness the disappearing act.

Judges 6:21
²¹Then the angel of the LORD reached out the tip of the staff that was in his hand and touched the meat and the unleavened cakes. And fire sprang up from the rock and consumed the flesh and the unleavened cakes. And the **angel** of the LORD **vanished from his sight**. (ESV)

Luke 21:31
³¹And their eyes were opened, and they recognized him. **And he vanished from their sight**. (ESV)

Elohim (many of them angels) can instantly and literally disappear as you look directly at them. I don't mean that they walked away and you lost sight of them. I mean they go from being visible one moment to becoming invisible in the blink of an eye.

Chapter 11

Angels Fornicated With Humans? So What?

- The enemy of God (Satan) wants to destroy ministry, break covenant, usurp authority steal from Christians and oppress Christians
- God is seeking to disclose some supernatural things
- To define, disclose and expose these angels
- To uncover the workings of a destructive force in the dark kingdom, God wants to reveal his answers and help humans
- To expose the obstacle that is hindering the Christians from receiving the fullness that God has for us…that is the Angels are implementing forceful or natural means intended to distract and deter Christians
- Uncovering the methods of the evil spirits will translate to the blessing of lives
- If we know how the enemy has operated in the past then we improve our understanding how he is operating now
- We must be knowledgeable, we must be willing to know the truth and we must be ready to do something with the truth we know
- Now is the time for the world to know their enemy
- This uncontested spirit has achieved tremendous success by stealing and misleading the lives of billions of humans. We cannot assume that God simply stops every plan of Satan because there have been times in history when God has not stopped the plan of Satan

(e.g. the Jewish holocaust, abortions, sexual abuse of children, murder of the innocent, suffering of orphans and widows, etc). It is a war…and wars require warriors.

- Revealing the dark prince will equip humans with facts to walk, considering God-given knowledge. We must not only be informed, but equipped to discern wickedness in all its shapes and forms.
- Our libraries are full of worthless books. The world education system is full of errors and myth; people believe myth but oppose the God of Genesis.

Satan was told to his face by Yahweh about the prophecy in Genesis 3:15. Much of the Old Testament is about the battles and struggles of Satan trying to prevent the prophecy of Genesis 3:15. And Satan's soldiers included not only the fallen elohim but also the offspring of the fallen elohim and even the offspring of Satan himself.

Genesis 3:14-15
¹⁴The Lᴏʀᴅ God said to the serpent, "Because you have done this, cursed are you above all livestock and above all beasts of the field; on your belly you shall go, and dust you shall eat all the days of your life. ¹⁵I will put enmity between you and the woman, and between YOUR offspring and her offspring; he shall bruise your head, and you shall bruise his heel." (ESV)

In Genesis 3:14, the word אֶל־הַנָּחָשׁ is the ancient Hebrew word that for some strange reason is translated into the English word Serpent. But notice how it has the letters אֶל in front of it. Those two letters in the front means that it is literally god-like because those two letters are "EL". As most of you already know, the serpent is actually Lucifer the light bearer who is also called Satan. Anyway, Yahweh said to the Serpent

114

"YOUR OFFSPRING", God literally meant the bloodline descendants of Satan himself. In other words, the serpent (the Nahash in Hebrew) was among the Beney-ha-elohim that had sexual intercourse with humans in Genesis 6:1-4 to birth the nephilim. Goliath, for example, had a mixture of human DNA and elohim DNA. And so the people that led the incursion to crucify Jesus Christ of Nazareth were descendants of the bloodline of the Nahash.

John 8:39-44

[39] They answered him, "Abraham is our father." Jesus said to them, "**If you were** Abraham's children, you would be doing what Abraham did, [40] but now you seek to kill me, a man who has told you the truth that I heard from God. This is not what Abraham did. [41] You are doing what **your father** did." They said to him, "We were not born of **sexual immorality**. We have one Father— even God." [42] Jesus said to them, "**If** God were your Father, you would love me, for I came from God and I am here. I came not of my own accord, but he sent me. [43] Why do you not understand what I say? It is because you cannot bear to hear my word. [44] You are of **your father the devil**, and your will is to do your father's desires. He was a murderer from the beginning, and has nothing to do with the truth, because there is no truth in him. When he lies, he speaks out of his own character, for he is a liar and the father of lies. (ESV)

Above we make a clear connection between Genesis 3:15 and John 8:44. Although I've never before heard anyone teaching this in any church nor any Bible study, I did not invent it. There it is in the Bible that you own. Above, in John chapter 8, we see that Jesus himself said that the devil is the father of the people seeking to kill him. Sometimes people tell me that they believe what the Bible says. Then I show them things they've never seen before and suddenly they want to debate with me. So I say to them, do you really believe the

Bible?...or just the parts that are in agreement with the erroneous doctrines that you've been taught since children's church. Folks, you will not graduate from the milk of the word to the meat of the word until you start reading the Bible with an open mind (open enough to believe everything it says). If you ignore parts of the Bible, you'll never get the full rich understanding of the message in that sacred holy book.

The great flood of Noah's time makes more sense when you understand that supernatural, non-humans which were called elohim (i.e. god's) tainted the human DNA by breeding with humans. Yahweh's plan to give rulership of this planet to his human imagers was under siege and nearly spoiled. That's why God drowned breastfeeding infants and weak widowed old ladies. How can you say that you serve a loving God without understanding why he'd drown the helpless old ladies, the innocent infants and everyone except Noah and his family? And how about the "infants" in the following verse?

1 Samuel 15:3
³ Now go and strike Amalek and devote to destruction all that they have. Do not spare them, but kill both man and woman, child **and infant**, ox and sheep, camel and donkey.'" (ESV)

The above verse includes children AND infants in the list of those to be killed. God's not trying to be redundant in that verse. Infants are different than children, which is why both are listed there. Infants are still breastfeeding. Why would Yahweh command the Israelites to also kill the innocent breastfeeding infants? How much sin have those breastfeeding infants committed that they deserve to ALL be killed? Many Christians will stumble through this question and fumble through the answer or simply say something like, "God has a

116

plan and sometimes we humans are not equipped to understand the mind of God". And of course, some Christians simply say, "I don't know". Well, if you study the Bible carefully, you'll notice that Amalek and the people in his township were direct descendants of the nephilim. In other words, they weren't human. Throughout the Bible, God helps the Israelites to exterminate the non-human DNA of the nephilim (e.g. David and Goliath). Only a small number of nephilim descendants survived.

So what happened to all the elohim that crossed the line by having sexual intercourse with humans? Let's see what the Bible says about those elohim.

> 1 Peter 3:18-20
> [18] For Christ also suffered once for sins, the righteous for the unrighteous, that he might bring us to God, being put to death in the flesh but made alive in the **spirit**, [19] **in which** he went and proclaimed to the **spirits** in prison, [20] because they formerly did not obey, **when** God's patience waited **in the days of Noah**, while the ark was being prepared, in which a few, that is, eight persons, were brought safely through water. (ESV)

They were jailed while God was waiting for the arc to be built. There are angels underground in this planet right now as I type this. And how do we know that this is underground here in this planet and not below the planet (as in south of the planet or some other part of the galaxy or in the heavens).

Ephesians 4:8-9

⁸ Therefore it says,
"When he ascended on high he led a host of captives, and he gave gifts to men." ⁹ In saying, "He ascended," what does it mean but that he had also descended **into the lower parts of the earth**? (ESV)

I believe that the Bible is the only book on the planet that is one hundred percent accurate and true. That is, the actual ancient Bible in its original form. That said, however, I believe there are many non-biblical texts that are reasonably close to accurate or at least somewhat close to the actual historical facts. And I think that many myths are at least inspired by actual historical facts. Although, most myths are probably heavily tainted and either intentionally altered to suit the needs of Satan or too far removed to be accurate. The Bible is not too far removed because it's the actual word of God whereas the non-biblical texts are the words of men or worse yet the deceiver (Satan). I say that to point out that there are many myths about deities being trapped deep under the surface of this planet. In the Greek myths, one of those places is called Tartarus.

2 Peter 2:4

⁴ For if God did not spare angels when they sinned, but cast them into **hell** and committed them to chains of gloomy darkness to be kept until the judgment; ⁵ if he did not spare the ancient world, but preserved Noah, a herald of righteousness, with seven others, when he brought a flood upon the world of the ungodly. (ESV)

Did you notice the word "Tartarus" in verse 4 above? That's because it's hidden behind the word "hell". Here's the same verse in the ancient Biblical Koine Greek.

2 Peter 2:4

⁴ ει γαρ ο θεος αγγελων αμαρτησαντων ουκ εφεισατο αλλα σειραις ζοφου **ταρταρωσας** παρεδωκεν εις κρισιν τετηρημενους (Greek, Textus Receptus)

Now you can clearly see the word Tartarus above which is underlined and bold. There are four ancient Biblical words hidden behind the word "hell" that mean at least four different things. They are Tartarus, Sheol, Hades and Gehenna. These four words are different because they refer to four separate and different locations. Yet translators have used the English word Hell for all four of those locations. Part of the confusion is kind of like what you might get with New York. When someone says New York, they might be talking about the City or the State. New York City is located within the state of New York. Tartarus is an area located inside of planet Earth under the surface of this planet and it's associated with the area called the "Bottomless Pit" which is also called the Abyss. The shaft that leads from the surface of planet Earth down into Tartarus will be unlocked in the end times to release the second beast in Revelation.

Revelation Chapter 9: verses 1-2, 11

¹And the fifth angel blew his trumpet, and I saw a star fallen from heaven to earth, and he was given the key to **the shaft of the bottomless pit**. ²He opened the shaft of the bottomless pit, and from the shaft rose smoke like the smoke of a great furnace, and the sun and the air were darkened with the smoke from the shaft.... ¹¹They have as king over them the angel of **the bottomless pit**. His name in Hebrew is Abaddon, and in Greek he is called Apollyon. (ESV)

This second beast is the one that will cause many people to receive the mark of the first beast. So it is the first beast whose name equates to 666 and that first beast is the main subject of this book.

So there's something in the lower parts of the earth. So why did Jesus descend into the lower parts of the Earth? It wasn't' to obtain a mineral sample. No, he went down there to make a proclamation in 1 Peter Ch3. Remember that every word and even every letter is significant in the Holy Scriptures of God. He went down to the lower parts of the earth (to Tartarus) to make a proclamation to those angels that tried to defeat the bloodline that God had created. Those "Son's of the Elohim" tried to defeat God's plan to have the messiah be born of a virgin human-woman of a certain blood line….a bloodline without the DNA of fallen angels. That was the bloodline of Abraham, Isaac, Jacob and Judah.

And what else do we see in Revelation nine one one, now we can see why people will be amazed that he "was", because Apollyon "was" walking the planet before the flood, he "was" in existence, he "is not", he is not here we do not see him any more he's gone into Tartarus, but he "will" come up out of the abyss, UP OUT OF THE ABYSS. Now that this is all coming out and becoming clear, up until now, we would just read over that, through it and not stop to think about it, it would just be one of those verses we read in the bible and we read a verse or two and we just kept going and we didn't stop even though we had no idea what we had just read. Well here's some of these verses that people read through and you don't think about them. Know we can understand. He was, he is not, and he will be again, he will come up out of the abyss. The abyss, the pit, the bottomless pit, Tartarus...all of these names are used for this place that Jesus had descended down into to make a proclamation to the angels...well he certainly didn't go down to make a proclamation to the minerals of the earth, the sand and the rocks, he made a proclamation to something to an intelligent entity that could understand the proclamation.

Do you think Jesus would go down there and make this proclamation to the lower ranking angels? I think he might have made this proclamation so that the angel who is the king of all the angels down there would clearly hear this proclamation. Well guess who that king angel would be...none other than the angel that will cause people to receive the mark of the beast. We can see that because in Rev 9:11 he is said to be the king over all the angels in the abyss.

Chapter 12

⚡ **The Beast**

Do we really believe what the Bible says? Or do we only believe it when it fits within our pre-existing belief system? Where in the Bible do people get this idea that the Holy Scriptures should NOT be taken literally? The Bible should be taken literally unless it is extremely obvious that it is not literal (the key word there is "extremely"). Satan would definitely NOT want us to take it literally because if we don't take it literal then it can mean anything that our creative minds needs it to mean. It is easier for Satan to influence us if we don't take it literally. Because if it doesn't mean what it actually says, then what does it mean? I've heard people say that the Bible means whatever the spirit tells you that it means. That doesn't work either because many different Christians have many different interpretations for each verse depending on who you talk to. Since it often happens that one Christian has an interpretation of a verse that is opposite of what another Christian believes, then we know that the Holy Spirit did not interpret that scripture for at least one of those Christians (and possibly neither received their interpretation from the Holy Spirit). The Holy Spirit would not tell one Christian something that is in direct opposition of what the Holy Spirit tells me or someone else.

Out of the thirty plus English translations, which of the Bible interpreters had the right spirit on their side. Some people think that the King James Version ("KJV") is the most accurate of them all. Some even think that the KJV is the ONLY one that is right. See chapter 5 for proof that the KJV has some significant and obvious errors in it. That said, however, I don't think any of the English translations got it all right. It's not possible because the ancient Bible languages cannot be perfectly translated into English, for several reasons. Translation problems can be found in all the English translations. I still like to read the KJV sometimes because many other parts of it are well done and worth including in your Bible study as a parallel study. Remember, there is only one version of the Bible that is one hundred percent accurate and that is the original ancient autographs (e.g. the very first time ever that Moses [or other Biblical prophets] put ink to paper with his own hands). See chapter 5 in this book for more on translation issues.

Ok, so you want to know the name of the 666-beast and his current location right? Now we will examine the verses that tell us about the two main beasts in Revelation. Follow along with me and hang in there because there's some things that have to be undone in our thinking. In other words, years worth of mud build up had to be removed from my windshield before I was able to see the topic of the 666-beast so clearly. The only writings anywhere on the planet that I believe to be completely accurate and true is the Bible (in its original ancient language). So I am not trying to get you to believe something that is not in the Bible. I am trying to get you to actually believe what the actual autographs literally say [[although there are no known autographs in the world today…scholars and interpreters can be very confident when attempting to reconstruct the autographs due to the enormous volumes of textual evidence available to scholars, interpreters, archaeologist, etc.]] Thank God he made it possible for us humans to be able to triangulate each and every letter of the autographs with a high degree of confidence. You know the saying, "you can't teach and old dog new tricks". Well, let's prove that saying wrong. I believe many of the readers of this book will be able to learn a new trick…namely, how to identify the name and current location of the 666-beast. Let's start by identifying some of the more common misconceptions about the 666-beast; All of the following are non-Biblical teachings.

1. That he is Thee <u>ONE</u> prophesied "antichrist" (i.e. all the attributes of THEE ONE antichrist are to be found in one sole being). That is implied by the way it has been previously taught.
2. That he will be a <u>HUMAN</u> that will become possessed by some evil spirit (some say possessed by Satan, the devil or some other very strong and very evil spirit).
3. That the 666-beast is a kingdom or an organization or a nation or a concept or something other than an actual individual being of flesh and blood (many animals and beasts have flesh and blood too).
4. That it is probably former president Obama or President Donald Trump or some future president of the USA or some other human world leader.
5. That it will be one of the Pope's (probably the next one if not this current one)

You've probably heard the debate regarding whether or not the book of Revelation was written in chronological order or not. Let's work on clearing that up. The book of Revelation was clearly not written in chronological order. Here's just one topic in Revelation that proves that.

Revelation 11:7

7 And when they have finished their testimony, **the beast** that rises **from the bottomless pit** will make war on them and conquer them and kill them, (ESV)

Revelation 13:01

And I saw a **beast rising out of the sea**, with ten horns and seven heads, with ten diadems on its horns and blasphemous names on its heads. (ESV)

Revelation 13:11

11 Then I saw another beast rising out of the earth. It had two horns like a lamb and it spoke like a dragon. **12** It exercises all the authority of **the first** beast in its presence, and makes the earth and its inhabitants worship the **first beast**, whose mortal wound was healed. (ESV)

The first beast is the one that comes up out of the sea having seven heads. That first beast is the subject of this book because it's the one whose name equates to 666. As you study Revelation more closely, you'll see even more evidence that the 666-beast which rises up out of the sea is the first beast. In Revelation, the first ever mention of this beast is Revelation 13:01. Yet somehow, the second beast to rise up out of the bottomless pit (i.e. Abyss) is mentioned BEFORE that in Revelation 11:07. Case closed, the book of Revelation is not written in chronological order. As you go on to study Revelation on your own, it will be helpful to keep in mind this convention in Revelation where not everything was written in chronological order. There is a little bit of jumping around at times, just like a typical conversation.

Let's unpack this a bit more. We'll start with the beast that causes people to receive the mark (i.e. 666 OR his name). This beast is actually the second beast to make his appearance in the end times (Bible says..."in that day"). We know that it is the second beast rather than the first beast by reading and following Revelation closely until chapter 13 verse 11 and 12.

Revelation 13:11-12
¹¹ Then I saw **another** beast rising out of the earth. It had two horns like a lamb and it spoke like a dragon. ¹² It exercises all the authority of the **first** beast in its presence, and makes the earth and its inhabitants worship the **first** beast, whose mortal wound was healed. (ESV)

The underlined words in bold font clarify whether it is the first or the second beast. To unpack the mystery of the antichrist, it is important to keep track of which beast the Bible is talking about each time a beast is mentioned in Revelation. The second beast is the one that rises up out of the Earth **NOT** out of the sea. The beast that rises up out of the sea is the first beast. Remember how earlier in this book we saw in the Bible that the Son's of God were imprisoned or bound up before the flood? (chapter 6) And we saw in the Bible that these prisons or locations are located here in planet Earth under the surface of this planet?

All the major players that have a very powerful role in Revelation are non-humans. Here are just some of them;

- The 1ˢᵗ beast that rises up from the sea having 7 heads; Revelation 13:01

- The 2nd beast (an angel aka "false prophet" that rises up out of the bottomless pit (i.e. Abyss) and causes earth dwellers to receive the mark of the first beast; Revelation 9:11
- The four angels that will kill a third of humans currently bound up at the Great River Euphrates; Revelation 9:14. Notice their prison is located here on planet Earth. So it should not be so unbelievable that other non-human beings might also have their prison located here on planet Earth.
- Satan is also called the ancient serpent, dragon and the devil; Revelation 20:02
- Seven angels blowing the seven trumpets; Revelation 8:02 through Revelation 11:15
- Seven angels with seven bowls; Revelation 15:07

There are more non-humans involved in major roles in the book of Revelation. All of the major pains to be dealt out to the humans will be administered and rendered by non-humans. The point is that with all these non-humans involved in the big roles, why do so many Christians think that the 666-beast must be a human. There's nothing at all in the Bible that indicates that the 666-beast is a human. Remember that Gabriel was called "the man Gabriel" in Daniel 9:21.

We saw that the "son's of God" in the old testament were non-humans (elohim). Well, one of those son's of God is the second beast that comes up out of the Earth. He comes up out of Tartarus. I know, this is so weird but let's take a closer look at the English translations of the Bible. By the way (as a side note), notice the only verse

128

number that reveals the name of the second beast, NINE ONE ONE (probably just an interesting coincidence).

Revelation 9:11
They have as king over them the <u>angel</u> of the bottomless pit. His name in Hebrew is Abaddon, and in Greek he is called <u>Apollyon</u>. (ESV)

Apollyon is the name of the second beast and he is clearly an angel (i.e. NOT human). But not just any angel, Apollyon is the angel of the bottomless pit and Apollyon is also a king above all other beings in the bottomless pit. Revelation 9:11 clearly rules out the possibility that the second beast is human. Apollyon is an elohim, an angel, and therefore a non-human. Several times in the Bible the word Beast comes up (over 200 times). And in every single case, the beast(s) that is being talked about has the following two (2) attributes; First of all, all beasts are non-human in the Bible. The second attribute of all beasts in the Bible is that they are a flesh and blood form that is physically touchable and visible to humans. In other words, a human doesn't have to enter into the spirit realm to observe a beast.

Exodus 8:18
The magicians tried by their secret arts to produce gnats, but they could not. So there were gnats on man and <u>beast</u>. (ESV)

Above is just one verse that reminds us of how that word "beast" is used. Exodus 8:18 would be senseless if it said "...So there were gnats on humans and humans." It would feel more like a typo. This shows us a clear distinction between humans and beasts. The Biblical Hebrew word that has been translated into the English word "man" is אָדָם which is often translated as mankind or human and is pronounced adam (ADM).

If you're still struggling to believe that the second beast is not human, then you're simply struggling to believe the bible. If you're not yet convinced that the second beast is an angel, then read Rev 9:11 again but much slower this time so that you can notice the word angel. So Apollyon is not human and he can take on the form of something that is flesh and blood. Apollyon (the second beast) is the one that causes everyone to receive the mark of the first beast. The following pericope (the word pericope means an extract from the Bible. In the English translations, a pericope often has a header, for example, "Jesus Heals A Paralytic" in Mathew 5:1. These headers are not in the original Bible, they were added by the translators)...well, the following pericope is important to follow slowly because a lot is lost in the translation from Greek to English. Below we will read this pericope in two different ways. First we will read it exactly as it is in the English Bible and after that we'll read it with some words that I will add to help clarify (i.e. like the Amplified Bible). But please check your Bible to confirm that the words I'm adding are simply to help differentiate the first beast from the second beast. My added words will be clearly marked like *[this]* (that is, enclosed in brackets, in italics and in a different font).

Here is the original ESV without my added words (just copy/pasted)

Revelation 13:11-18

¹¹ Then I saw another beast rising out of the earth. It had two horns like a lamb and it spoke like a dragon. ¹² It exercises all the authority of the first beast in its presence, and makes the earth and its inhabitants worship the first

beast, whose mortal wound was healed. [13] It performs great signs, even making fire come down from heaven to earth in front of people, [14] and by the signs that it is allowed to work in the presence of the beast it deceives those who dwell on earth, telling them to make an image for the beast that was wounded by the sword and yet lived. [15] And it was allowed to give breath to the image of the beast, so that the image of the beast might even speak and might cause those who would not worship the image of the beast to be slain. [16] Also it causes all, both small and great, both rich and poor, both free and slave, to be marked on the right hand or the forehead, [17] so that no one can buy or sell unless he has the mark, that is, the name of the beast or the number of its name. [18] This calls for wisdom: let the one who has understanding calculate the number of the beast, for it is the number of a man, and his number is 666. ("ESV")

The above is exactly a copy and paste from the ESV. The following is the same exact pericope but with my words added (in this book, anytime I add words to a Bible verse it will be very clear because my words will be italicized, in brackets AND in a different font...*[like this]*. Plus, since this book is inherently hard to believe, I'll clearly highlight it so that it's obviously different. I want it to be very clear that I don't have the intent of deceiving anyone. The topic of this book is so weird that it could make some people think that I'm trying to start a new cult religion. So I don't want to make it even weirder by making it seem like I'm adding words to the Bible with the intent to deceive. In this book, if something quoted from the Bible is **ONLY** underlined (or underlined and capitalized...**LIKE THIS**) then it is not something I added...rather it is just to highlight it. I think when you see it, most people will agree that it's easy to tell the difference between the words of the Bible and the ones I added. Lastly, if in doubt, please open your Bible and double check it (after all, we are supposed to be reading our Bibles, right?).

Revelation 13:11-18

[11] Then I saw another beast [*the second one*] rising out of the earth. It had two horns like a lamb and it spoke like a dragon. [12] It exercises all the authority of the first beast in its presence, and makes the earth and its inhabitants worship the first beast, whose mortal wound was healed. [13] It [*the second beast*] performs great signs, even making fire come down from heaven to earth in front of people, [14] and by the signs that it [*the second beast*] is allowed to work in the presence of the [*first*] beast it deceives those who dwell on earth, telling them to make an image for the [*first*] beast that was wounded by the sword and yet lived. [15] And it [*the second beast*] was allowed to give breath to the image of the [*first*] beast, so that the image of the [*first*] beast might even speak and might cause those who would not worship the image of the [*first*] beast to be slain. [16] Also it [*the second beast*] causes all, both small and great, both rich and poor, both free and slave, to be marked on the right hand or the forehead, [17] so that no one can buy or sell unless he has the mark, that is, the name of the [*first*] beast or the number of its name [*the name of the first beast*]. [18] This calls for wisdom: let the one who has understanding calculate the number of the [*first*] beast, for it is the number of a man, and his number is 666. ("ESV")

So you see, the first beast is the one whose name or number will be marked on peoples hand or forehead. The second beast ("Apollyon") is the one who causes people to receive the mark of the first beast. This is not an opinion, it is clear in the Greek because the Greek grammar rules make it unmistakable. To confirm this for yourself, I recommend that you do a little basic study of the Greek cases (nominative case, accusative case, and etcetera). Furthermore, you might find it helpful to study some of the basic Greek grammar rules that show you what to do when the English translations use a pronoun like the word "IT" or the word "HE". Because it can be a little confusing in English to figure out which noun is being replaced by the word

"IT". As an example, take a look at Revelation 13:13 in various English versions to see that some translations use the word "IT" while others use the word "HE" in reference to the second beast. But one English translation does it differently. Here's the "Good News Translation".

Revelation 13:13
¹³ **This second beast** performed great miracles; it made fire come down out of heaven to earth in the sight of everyone. (Good News Translation, "GNT")

We can now narrow down the field a little because we now can see that Apollyon is not the 666-beast. Instead, the first beast that comes up out of the sea is the 666-beast. In other words, the beast whose name and number is 666 is the first beast that comes up out of the sea. So the one that many call the "antichrist" is the first beast that comes up out of the sea and has the name and number of 666. If the second beast is a non-human that is mentioned in Greek Mythology, then perhaps the first beast is also a non-human that is also mentioned in Greek mythology. Why would God go out of his way to give us the name of the second beast in two (2) very different languages…hmmm.

Of course, we saw earlier in chapter 1 that it is a misnomer to call the first beast the antichrist. So that is why I often call him the 666-beast (and later in this book I will reveal his real name). If after reading this book, Bible teachers continue to call the 666-beast "the antichrist", then we continue to contribute to the deception and advance Satan's agenda to keep the world blind about the true identity of the 666-beast. No one should anymore be called "the antichrist". Prior to this book, you and I were calling him the antichrist because we didn't know any better. But now you know because you saw it in the Bible. My prayer is that more and more Christians will become informed about the true identity of the 666-beast so that more people will become undeceived about the end times prophecies.

Some people say to me, why should I care about the identity of the 666-beast? They say, I'm going to be raptured so I don't need to worry about the 666-beast at all. They say, it's not important so don't try to scare me with all this nonsense. To say that, is to say that some of God's word is not important and perhaps God wasted his time by putting this beast stuff in the Bible. The word Beast appears forty (40) times in the book of Revelation. Is the book of Revelation unimportant? Here's the first three verses of Revelation.

Revelation 1:1-3
¹ **The revelation of Jesus Christ, which God gave him to show to his servants the things that must soon take place. He made it known by sending his angel to his servant John, ² who bore witness to the word of God and to the testimony of Jesus Christ, even to all that he saw. ³ Blessed is the one who reads aloud the words of this prophecy, and blessed are those who hear, and who keep what is written in it, for the time is near.** (ESV)

If it seems like this topic about the beast is unimportant, notice that God gave this revelation to Jesus Christ and it says that the one who reads the words of this prophecy out loud will be <u>blessed</u>. The ones that hear it and keep it will also be <u>blessed</u>. That's how important the book of Revelation is to God. What other books in the Bible does God promise blessings for, if you read it out loud? And what other books does God promise blessings for if you hear and keep what is written in it? So let us not think that the beast topic is

134

unimportant. I can see why Satan would want humans to think that Revelation is not important.

Notice that the Bible gives us two different names for the second beast. One of the reasons that two different names are given is because there are two main languages involved in the scriptures. Furthermore, Hebrew and Greek were very common among the Israelites of that region. In other words, the Old Testament was written in an ancient form of Hebrew while the New Testament was written in first century Koine Greek[5]. It makes sense that different civilizations with different languages would have different names for the same being. How do you pronounce Jesus in Spanish? How about Jesus in Chinese or Russian? Even though the name of Jesus (our lord and savior) is the same person for the Chinese as for the Russians the name is pronounced and spelled differently. The Chinese do not use English letters to write the name of Jesus. In Greek Jesus is spelled Ἰησοῦς. I'm pointing out these different names for the second beast because it helps to see that the first beast has different names too, depending on which civilization is writing about the 666-beast. And if the second beast is an elohim (i.e. an angel), then the first beast might also be an elohim. Not all elohim's are angels and not all angels are the same. The word elohim means a being whose natural habitat is the unseen supernatural realm and therefore not human (see Chapter 4 for more on the word elohim). In the unseen supernatural realm there are various kinds of beings. We are now closing in on the identity of the 666-beast. And yes, we will know the current location and the name of the 666-beast, the one they mistakenly call the "antichrist".

---

[5] There seems to be some possibility that some or all of the New Testament autographs were written in Hebrew or Aramaic with no Greek at all. Furthermore, some scholars believe that Aramaic is a very ancient version or dialect of Hebrew)

Our next step in unpacking this is to look at all the portions of the Bible that are talking about the 666-beast. So below I have extracted just the parts of the Bible that are talking about the 666-beast so we can see everything the Bible has to say about the first beast that comes up out of the sea. Here below, I have taken all the Bible verses about the 666-beast from various different books of the Bible and assembled together without the name of the book nor the chapter, nor the verse numbers. Here it is.

Let those curse it who curse the day,
who are ready to rouse up Leviathan.
Can you draw out Leviathan with a fishhook
or press down his tongue with a cord? Can you put a rope in his nose
or pierce his jaw with a hook? Will he **make many pleas to you**? Will he **speak to you soft words**? Will he **make a covenant with you** to take him for your servant forever? Will you play with him as with a bird, or will you put him on a leash for your girls? Will traders bargain over him?
Will they divide him up among the merchants? Can you fill **his skin** with harpoons or his head with fishing spears? **Lay your hands on him; remember the battle—you will not do it again**! Behold, **the hope of a man is false**; he is **laid low even at the sight of him**. **No one** is so fierce that he dares to stir him up. Who then is he who **can stand before me**? Who has first given to me, that I should repay him? Whatever is under the whole heaven is mine. **I will not keep silence** concerning his limbs, or his mighty strength, or his goodly frame. Who can strip off his outer garment? Who would come near him with a bridle? Who can open the doors of his face?
Around his teeth is terror. His back is made of rows of shields, shut up closely as with a seal. One is so near to another that no air can come between them. They are joined one to another;
they clasp each other and cannot be separated. **His sneezings flash forth light**, and his eyes are like the eyelids of the dawn. Out of his mouth go **flaming torches**; **sparks of fire** leap forth. Out of his **nostrils** comes forth **smoke**, as from a boiling pot and burning rushes. His breath kindles **coals**, and **a flame comes forth from**

136

his mouth. In his neck abides strength, and terror dances before him. The folds of his **flesh** stick together, firmly cast on him and immovable. His **heart is hard as a stone**, hard as the lower millstone. **When he raises himself up the mighty are afraid**; at the crashing **they are beside themselves**. Though the sword reaches him, it does not avail, nor the spear, the dart, or the javelin. He counts iron as straw, and bronze as rotten wood. The arrow cannot make him flee; for him sling stones are turned to stubble. Clubs are counted as stubble;
he laughs at the rattle of javelins. His underparts are like sharp potsherds; he spreads himself like a threshing sledge on the mire. He makes **the deep** boil like a pot; he makes **the sea** like a pot of ointment. Behind him he leaves a shining wake; one would think the deep to be white-haired.
On earth there is not his like, a creature without fear. **He sees everything that is high**; **he is king over all the sons of pride**.

"Son of man, raise a lamentation over Pharaoh king of Egypt and say to him:
"   You consider yourself a lion of the nations,
          but you are like **a dragon in the seas**;
          you burst forth in your rivers,
          trouble the waters with your feet,
          and foul their rivers.

Yet God my King is from of old, working salvation in the midst of the earth. You divided the sea by your might; you **broke the heads of the sea monsters on the waters**. **You crushed the heads of Leviathan; you gave him as food for the creatures of the wilderness**. You split open springs and brooks; you dried up ever-flowing streams. Yours is the day, yours also the night; you have established the heavenly lights and the sun. You have fixed all the boundaries of the earth; you have made summer and winter.

Here is **the sea**, great and wide, which teems with creatures innumerable, living things both small and great. There go the ships, **and Leviathan**, which you formed to play in it.

137

Your dead shall live; their bodies shall rise. You who dwell in the dust, awake and sing for joy! For your dew is a dew of light, and **the earth will give birth to the dead**. Come, my people, enter your chambers, and shut your doors behind you; hide yourselves for a little while until the fury has passed by. For behold, the Lord is coming out from his place to punish the inhabitants of the earth for their iniquity, and the earth will disclose the blood shed on it, and will no more cover its slain. **In that day** the Lord with his hard and great and strong sword **will punish Leviathan the fleeing serpent, Leviathan the twisting serpent, and he will slay the dragon that is in the sea. In that day**, A pleasant vineyard, sing of it! I, the Lord, am its keeper; every moment I water it. Lest anyone punish it, I keep it night and day; I have no wrath. Would that I had thorns and briers to battle! I would march against them, I would burn them up together. Or let them lay hold of my protection, let them make peace with me, let them make peace with me. In **days to come** Jacob shall take root, Israel shall blossom and put forth shoots and fill the whole world with fruit. Has he struck them as he struck those who struck them? Or have they been slain as their slayers were slain? Measure by measure, by exile you contended with them; he removed them with his fierce breath in the day of the east wind. Therefore by this the guilt of Jacob will be atoned for, and this will be the full fruit of the removal of his sin: when he makes all the stones of the altars like chalkstones crushed to pieces, no Asherim or incense altars will remain standing. For the fortified city is solitary, a habitation deserted and forsaken, like the wilderness; there the calf grazes; there it lies down and strips its branches. When its boughs are dry, they are broken; women come and make a fire of them. For this is a people without discernment; therefore he who made them will not have compassion on them; he who formed them will show them no favor. In that day from the river Euphrates to the Brook of Egypt the Lord will thresh out the grain, and you will be gleaned one by one, O people of Israel. And **in that day a great trumpet will be blown**, and those who were lost in the land of Assyria and those who were driven out to the land of Egypt will come and worship the Lord on the holy mountain at Jerusalem.

And I saw a beast rising out of **the sea**, with ten horns and seven heads, with ten diadems on its horns and blasphemous names on its heads.

And the beast that I saw was like a leopard; its feet were like a bear's, and its mouth was like a lion's mouth. And to it the dragon gave his power and his throne and great authority.

One of its heads seemed to have a mortal wound, but its mortal wound was healed, and the whole earth marveled as they followed the beast.

And they worshiped the dragon, for he had given his authority to the beast, and they worshiped the beast, saying, "**Who is like the beast, and who can fight against it**?"

And the beast was given a mouth uttering haughty and blasphemous words, and it was allowed to exercise authority for forty-two months.

It exercises all the authority of the first beast in its presence, and makes the earth and its inhabitants worship the first beast, whose **mortal** wound was healed.

and by the signs that it is allowed to work in the presence of the beast it deceives those who dwell on earth, telling them to make an image for the beast that was wounded by the sword and yet lived.

And it was allowed to give breath to the image of the beast, so that the image of the beast might even speak and might cause those who would not worship the image of the beast **to be slain**.

so that no one can buy or sell unless he has the mark, that is, the name of the beast or the number of its name.

This calls for wisdom: let the one who has understanding calculate the number of the beast, for it is the number of a man, and his number is 666

And another angel, a third, followed them, saying with a loud voice, "If anyone worships the beast and its image and receives a mark on his forehead or on his hand

And the smoke of their torment goes up forever and ever, and they have no rest, day or night, these worshipers of the beast and its image, and whoever receives the mark of its name."

And I saw what appeared to be a sea of glass mingled with fire—and also those who had conquered the beast and its image and the number of its name, standing beside the sea of glass with harps of God in their hands.

So the first angel went and poured out his bowl on the earth, and harmful and painful sores came upon the people who bore the mark of the beast and worshiped its image.

The fifth angel poured out his bowl on the throne of the beast, and its kingdom was plunged into darkness. People gnawed their tongues in anguish

And I saw, coming out of the mouth of the dragon and out of the mouth of the beast and out of the mouth of the false prophet, three unclean spirits like frogs.

And he carried me away in the Spirit into a wilderness, and I saw a woman sitting on a scarlet beast that was full of blasphemous names, and it had seven heads and ten horns.

But the angel said to me, "Why do you marvel? I will tell you the mystery of the woman, and of the beast with seven heads and ten horns that carries her.
The beast that you saw was, and is not, and is about to rise from the bottomless pit and go to destruction. And the dwellers on earth whose names have not been written in the book of life from the foundation of the world will marvel to see the beast, because it was and is not and is to come.

As for the beast that was and is not, it is an eighth but it belongs to the seven, and it goes to destruction.

And the ten horns that you saw are ten kings who have not yet received royal power, but they are to receive authority as kings for one hour, together with the beast.

These are of one mind and hand over their power and authority to the beast.

And the ten horns that you saw, they and the beast will hate the prostitute. They will make her desolate and naked, and devour her flesh and burn her up with fire,

for God has put it into their hearts to carry out his purpose by being of one mind and handing over their royal power to the beast, until the words of God are fulfilled.

And he called out with a mighty voice, " Fallen, fallen is Babylon the great! She has become a dwelling place for demons, a haunt for every unclean spirit, a haunt for every unclean bird, a haunt for every unclean and detestable beast.

And I saw the beast and the kings of the earth with their armies gathered to make war against him who was sitting on the horse and against his army.

And **the beast was captured**, and with it the false prophet who in its presence had done the signs by which he deceived those who had received the mark of the beast and those who worshiped its image. These two were **thrown alive into the lake of fire** that burns with sulfur.

Then I saw thrones, and seated on them were those to whom the authority to judge was committed. Also I saw the souls of those who had been beheaded for the testimony of Jesus and for the word of God, and who had not worshiped the beast or its image and had not received its mark on their foreheads or their hands. They came to life and reigned with Christ for a thousand years.

and the devil who had deceived them was thrown into the lake of fire and sulfur where the beast and the false prophet were, and they will be tormented day and night forever and ever.

Would it make sense that the most high God has interacted with the 666-beast in the ancient past? In fact, God and the 666-beast have had significant interaction before the flood. God created Leviathan (Psalm 104:26). The name of the 666-beast is Leviathan in ancient Hebrew. The current location of Leviathan is here in planet earth under the depth of the sea (in the deep, as the Bible says). In ancient Hebrew Leviathan is spelled as follows;

לויתן

NTYVL

Keep in mind that Hebrew is read from right to left (i.e. backwards compared to English). Therefore, if Hebrew letters were placed around a circle, we would likely have to read the letters in the circle counterclockwise instead of clockwise. Here's how the Hebrew Bible spells Leviathan.

L = ל

V = ו

Y = י

T = ת

N = ן

Also keep in mind that the ancient Hebrew Bible does not contain vowels (i.e. A, E, I, O, U). If you were to remove the vowels in the English transliteration it would look like LVYTN. To transliterate his name into English you would add vowels to help pronounce it. When you add the vowels you get

LeViYaThaN

Satan also had interaction with Leviathan. Satan also understands the Bible very well. So now you can see why the Satanic Bible has the name of Leviathan on the cover. Here's a photo of the cover of the Satanic Bible (Note: the first image is unedited while the second image has white letters that I added to show the corresponding letter in the English alphabet).

I was a little frightened the first time that I realized that those were Hebrew letters on the cover of the Satanic Bible. And it suddenly dawned on me that the spelling used on the cover of the Satanic bible is the same exact spelling used in the ancient Hebrew Bible (i.e. LVYTN). Remember you have to read it backwards and it starts at the bottom of the pentagram and it goes counterclockwise (i.e. backwards). Start reading at the six o'clock position going counterclockwise.

In the following photo of the Satanic Bible, I added the white letter of the English alphabet going counterclockwise as an aid to help you see the name LVYTN.

Many Bible scholars are extremely intelligent. So the fact that misinterpretations about the 666-beast have been widespread is not because they lacked intelligence. And I don't believe that prior Bible scholars (also; preachers, priests, teachers, evangelists and pastors) were intentionally trying to deceive their congregations. I believe that prior Bible scholars have been unable to discern the name and current location of the 666-beast because God has a perfect plan including the timing of everything. Now is the time for you to know the name and the current location of the 666-beast. Prior generations of Christians have passed away and therefore had no need to know. However, the time is at hand and Leviathan is about to rise up out of the Sea.

Daniel 12:04
But you, Daniel, shut up the words and seal the book, until the time of the end. Many shall run to and fro, and <u>knowledge shall increase</u>." (ESV)

Many who are alive today will be alive to witness this mega beast with their own eyes (Note: Did you notice how I avoided the topic of the rapture? Yeah, the rapture is an entire book unto itself so be on the lookout for another book in the future...I found something stunning in the ancient Bible language about the rapture...that no one is talking about for some strange reason). Meanwhile, God is revealing some information about the 666-beast in order that some might not be deceived and be able to conquer Leviathan and his partner Apollo.

Revelation 15:02
And I saw what appeared to be a sea of glass mingled with fire—and also those who had <u>conquered the beast</u> and its image and the number of its name, standing beside the sea of glass <u>with harps of God in their hands</u>. (ESV)

Some peoples are going to have to "conquer" the 666-beast in order for the above prophecy to be fulfilled. In the prophecy of Revelation 15:02, the ones that conquer the beast will afterwards be standing beside the sea of glass with harps of God in their hands. How will they be able to conquer the beast and not be deceived? Not everyone who sees the beast will be able to conquer the beast. Many who see Apollyon and Leviathan will worship the beast. And those that worship the beast will not be saved.

Although you might not yet be fully convinced, at this point in this book, we can at least start feeling reasonably comfortable with the possibility that Leviathan is the name of the 666-beast. It is at least the name used in the Old Testament for the 666-beast. In other ancient civilizations, Leviathan was called Tannin, Titan, Yam (also Yam Yam Yam, which is abbreviated YYY, which if you use the Hebrew letters for YYY that is 666). In Greek mythology (where we also find Apollyon, Leviathan's partner in crime), Leviathan is called Teitan. In gematria, Teitan equates to 666 when using the Greek letters (300+5+10+300+1+50=666).

However, there is still more evidence in the Bible. That is, of course, if you actually believe what the Bible says. The Bible is NOT the "inspired" word of God but rather the actual exact word of God himself. This idea of the Bible being the "inspired" word of God is from Satan. Yes, I said from Satan. It is a lie, a strong deception and a very slick move by the powers that oppose Jesus Christ. I'm not saying that your pastor is trying to deceive you if he calls it the "inspired" word of God. He's probably not trying to deceive you but he himself has been deceived just like I was deceived.

148

In fact, I'm pretty sure there's still some things that I myself continue to be deceived about. God is continuously clearing things up for me to gradually undo the deception that I was previously brought up in. Unless one has a perfect and complete understanding of the entire word of God, there's some likelihood that at least some deception is at work. I know it's a harsh word but why do I call it deception, because God is not the one that wants us to lack clarity in his scriptures. In other words if your pastor calls it "inspired", he is lovingly trying to teach you what he was taught to believe. He means well. But Satan is the current ruler of this world and Satan controls all the significant institutions of this world including most Bible colleges.

That is why someone can graduate from a Bible college with a Masters or a PhD in divinity or theology and come out of college convinced that the Bible is NOT the actual exact word of God but rather just the "inspired" word of God [[and for you scholars out there who are lurking into my book; i) thank you for reading my book and, ii) I'm talking about the Autographs being the actual exact word of God, iii) because we all know that none of the English translations are a hundred percent accurate]]. You see, if Satan can get us to believe that the Bible is not the very exact word of God himself, then he successfully brings us a step closer to bending the word of God. And if we're allowed to bend the word of God, then how far can we bend it. If the Bible is nothing more than words written by a human (a human whose writing was "inspired" by God), then the words in the Bible are easier to bend. And that is exactly what many humans do. They bend it and mold it such that it fits better within their pre-existing beliefs.

Why wouldn't the Bible say what it means? And why wouldn't the Bible mean what it says?

I beg you, please pause for a moment right now to focus on the previous sentence. Why would God try to trick us by telling us things that are not accurate? God didn't trick us. He's not trying to trick us…it's all there in the Bible. Satan is the one that has been tricking us. Remember, there is a struggle (Ephesians 6:12). Love your pastors and pray for them because they are being attacked by invisible beings that have supernatural powers that actually exist. Probably most of what your pastor is teaching you is accurate. And thank God that we don't have to have a perfect understanding of the Bible in order for us to be saved and have eternal life through Jesus Christ. All we need for salvation is to believe that Jesus Christ is the ONLY way to eternal life because Jesus Christ is the ONLY way to the heavenly father. And to ONLY worship Jesus Christ and his heavenly father of whom Jesus also said that he and the father are one….key word there is "ONLY".

John 14:6-7
⁶ Jesus said to him, "I am **the way**, and the truth, and **the life**. **No one** comes to the Father except through me. ⁷ If you had known me, you would have known my Father also. From now on you do know him and have **seen him**." (ESV)

John 10:30
I and the father are one. ("ESV")

Jesus Christ and his Heavenly Father are one. So much so that all of creation was done through Jesus Christ including the creation of this earth and the plants in it, as well as the creation of Adam. Jesus Christ our lord and savior did not begin his existence two thousand years ago at the virgin birth. It might take a whole n'other book to convince people that Jesus existed long before he manifested into human flesh and blood form. Jesus Christ actually was there at the Exodus event, in the burning bush and many other scenes in the Old Testament. They just didn't call him Jesus Christ yet because he had not yet manifested into the promised messiah. Read the book of John and notice that the word "him" in the following verse is referring to Jesus Christ.

John 1:3
All things were made through <u>him</u>, and without him was <u>not any thing</u> made that was made. ("ESV")

Anyway, that was my altar call just in case you missed it. And I just revealed the secret to eternal life. Well, eternal life is really not a secret for many humans. But somehow, it is still a secret to many that call themselves Christians. I know that many Catholics do not yet know that we ought not pray to anyone except to Jesus Christ (or through Jesus Christ) because a human cannot get to the Heavenly Father except through Jesus Christ...not the Catholic priest, not the virgin Mary, not Saint Peter nor Saint Paul nor any other human that has ever lived except through Jesus Christ alone.

Matthew 23:9
And do not call anyone on earth 'father,' for you have one Father, and he is in heaven. (NIV)

Anyway, I digress. But back to Leviathan and the fact that we can gleam from the Bible that he's the same being as the

151

666-beast of Revelation. Read Isaiah to notice that the following verse is talking about the end times.

Isaiah 27:1
In that day the Lord with his hard and great and strong sword will punish **Leviathan** the fleeing serpent, **Leviathan** the twisting serpent, and he will slay **the dragon that is in the sea**. ("ESV")

Which dragon that is currently in the sea is God going to slay in the end times? The book of Revelation tells us exactly which dragon from the sea is going to be slain by God. In Revelation, that dragon is the one with seven heads whose name has the number of 666. So how come LVYTN doesn't add up to 666. Because the Old Testament calls him LVYTN but he has several names including but not limited to

- Teitan (in gematria is 666)
- Tannin
- Titan
- Lotan
- Yam Yam Yam (YYY = 666)
- Poseidon
- Neptune
- Leviathan
- Litanu
- Liwya

From all around the world, there are several artifacts, carvings, writings, drawings and other items from ancient times through which the ancients communicated to us what they believed to be true about a seven headed dragon. When they wrote about it or depicted it, they were not trying to create a work of fiction. They were literally recording actual history.

Mesopotamian iconography from about 3,000 years BC shows a seven headed dragon that was defeated by God. And around 1928AD, a massive ancient library was found in the Northern region of modern day Syria. This region was called Ugarit. The Ugaritic literature contained the Ras Shamra tablets which archeologists dated from around 1400BC to around 1200BC. The clay tablets found in that Ugarit Library mention the grandfather of Abraham, the Israelite tribe of Zebulon and several other topics that are in the Hebrew Bible. Much is said in Ugarit literature about a great seven headed dragon. Ugarit tablets also describe an ancient war between an elohim and that seven-headed dragon. In the Ras Shamra tables of ancient Ugarit, the seven-headed dragon was called Litanu or Lotan. Ugaritic tablets speak of the dragon as literally having seven heads. One of the ancient Ugaritic drawings was drawn with spots throughout the torso of the dragon. So, not only was the Ugaritic dragon drawn with seven heads, but it's skin pattern was drawn like that of the fur of a leopard.

Revelation 13:2 was written during the first century AD, shortly after the resurrection of Jesus Christ. Roughly two thousand years before Revelation was written, a drawing was made of the beast described in Revelation 13:1-4. Leviathan is also mentioned in later Jewish literature including a book found among the Dead Sea Scrolls (1 Enoch). So if you think that Leviathan is a myth about some seven headed dragon that never actually existed, than maybe other parts of the Bible are also just a myth, right? Oh, well then how is it that you get to pick which parts of the Bible are myth and which parts are not myth. Why would God dedicate so much of the Bible to a description about something that never actually existed? Why are so many eschatologists (i.e. end times scholars) in disagreement about the end times. And why are so many eschatologists unclear or even confused about the end times prophecies.

Maybe if Bible scholars started actually believing what the Bible actually says, then maybe they'd understand the end times events a little better. Actually, once I changed my view of the Bible such that I now take it literally and believe every word of it, I can better understand most of what I read. I recommend you clear out and purge your brain so that you can start fresh with a blank sheet of paper. After you fully clear off all the pre-existing beliefs (which is very hard to do, but through God all things are possible)…well, after that, you will see many awesome things in the Bible and you'll feel like you can finally understand it. After all, who would you rather believe, the Bible (which is the actual exact word of God) or the teachings of a mere human? I'll take the word of God over the word of ANY human all day long. By the way, a prophet is not just anyone that claims to be a prophet. A prophet (as seen in the Bible) is someone that God selected and literally met with in person and God asked him to relay a message to the humans. A real prophet actually hears the voice of God (audibly, out loud and clear) and also sees a small dose of the glory of God.

Chapter 13

🐂 **Biblical Evidence**

Here is a list of some of the strongest pieces of Biblical evidence that prove the claims in this book about Leviathan.

1. Isaiah 27:1 **In that day the Lᴏʀᴅ with his hard and great and strong sword will punish Leviathan the fleeing serpent, Leviathan the twisting serpent, and he will slay the dragon that is in the sea**.

   a. How silly is it to think that this verse is talking about the most high God slaying a mere crocodile or a mere hippopotamus or any species from the commonly known animal kingdom. No, Yahweh is not going to slay a whale either. Why does Isaiah tell us that God will use his "**hard** and **great** and **strong sword** to punish **Leviathan**"? Will Yahweh really need such intense weaponry to slay a crocodile or a whale? Erase your brain and start reading the Bible with a fresh new mind…a mind that is newly prepared to believe every word of the Bible. In the above verse, notice the timing of when this prophecy is to take place. It will happen in "that day", which is in the end times. You only have to read the parts that surround this verse to confirm for yourself that this verse is talking about the end times. Is it sinking in yet? Where else in the Bible do we see a dragon that is in the sea? In Revelation, of course. And where else in the Bible do we see God slaying a dragon that (in the time of Isaiah) was in the sea? At the time of the writing of

Isaiah, the dragon was still in the sea. That's why it says "the dragon that **is** in the sea". I believe that Leviathan the dragon is probably still prevented and bound in the sea that Isaiah was talking about. Based on the non-Biblical evidence, the region in which the "mythical" seven headed dragon was located reached from Egypt to the northern parts of the Middle East. That region from which the sea-beast will likely rise up is the most heavily guarded region on planet earth. The US military machine has been intensely controlling the Middle East for some time now. Virtually all of the world's conflicts have the Middle East as their epicenter. As if Satan had his people on standby awaiting the return of Leviathan or perhaps working on making his rising-up happen sooner. In Job 3:8 we learn that some are skilled at rousing up supernatural beings. A type of conjurer or sorcerer. Here's Job 3:8 in two different English translations;

    i. Job 3:8 **Let those curse it who curse the day, who are skilled in rousing up Leviathan.** (Amplified Bible)

    ii. Job 3:8 **Tell the sorcerers to curse that day, those who know how to control Leviathan.** (The Good News Translation)

2. Job 41:25 **When he <u>raises himself up</u> the <u>mighty</u> are <u>afraid</u>; at the crashing they are <u>beside themselves</u>.**

    a. The key word in this verse is "<u>**mighty**</u>". That word in the ancient Bibblical Hebrew is אלים (pronounced elym or elim or alym). Recall that elohim is the Biblical Hebrew word which is translated into the word God, which in Hebrew is אלהים . Notice how similar those two Hebrew words are. The only difference is the letter ה .

But the fact that there is only a one letter difference, is not the only clue that both of those words speak of non-humans that are actually divine heavenly beings (look at table 13.1 later in this chapter for a word study of אלים). That table is important because it proves that the mighty are not human but rather gods (i.e. divine beings of the supernatural realm). So the "**mighty**" in Job 41:25 are divine heavenly beings that are super natural and NOT human. And the one that **raises himself up** in this verse is Leviathan. This verse is NOT telling us that the elym become afraid and beside themselves when they see a crocodile rise up. This verse proves that Leviathan is not a mere crocodile nor any other member of the commonly known animal kingdom. Elym (אלים) are non-human, divine heavenly beings with such supernatural powers that they would never become afraid and beside themselves at the uprising of a crocodile (nor any member of the commonly known animal kingdom). This verse (Job 41:25) lets us know that Leviathan is not a myth. Why would the divine heavenly beings become so afraid of something that doesn't exist? Obviously, Leviathan exists and obviously he is so intensely frightful that even the gods are beside themselves. Something had prevented me from seeing this until I was forty years old. I feel like I lived forty years with blind folds on.

3. Job 41:4 **Will he make a covenant with you to take him for your servant forever?**
   a. Wait. Did he just say "**covenant**"? The oldest book in the Bible has this verse where Yahweh is prophetically asking Job if Leviathan will make a covenant in the future. How can people continue to think that Leviathan might not be an actual being that exists? This is an intense and serious conversation that Yahweh is having with Job. This verse (Job 41:4) show us that Leviathan does exist. Furthermore, it shows us that he can't possibly be a mere crocodile or a hippo because Leviathan is capable of entering into a covenant with humans. How can it possibly make any sense for God to ask Job something like...[will a non-existent mythical being make a covenant with you]...or something like...[will a crocodile make a covenant with you].

4. Job 41:8 **Lay your hands on him; remember the battle—you will not do it again!**
   a. Although I'm not sure on this verse, I think it's possible that the word "**remember**" is talking about the battle that occurred before the flood which led to Leviathan being imprisoned in the sea. In many ancient sources outside of the Bible, there was an intensely mega battle between the gods which included a seven headed dragon that was defeated by the highest god. Most English interpretations treat this verse as if God was saying to Job that if he dares to touch Leviathan that the battle would be so memorable (in a bad way) that Job would never do it again. I'm not convinced either way. After this book is published, I plan to

158

dig deeper into the Hebrew on this verse so please check the companion website for potential updates.

5. Job 41:9 Behold, **the hope** of a man is false; he is laid low **even at the sight** of him.

   a. Even just the sight of Leviathan is enough to make humans hopeless and laid low. Is this talking about the Roman empire? Obviously NOT, just read that verse real slow again and see if the Roman empire is in view. I've seen elephants before. I've even seen crocodiles and alligators. And yes, I have even seen hippos and whales. None of those animals made me lose hope and none of those animals made me laid low (by the way, "laid low" means to be cast down, defeated, or overwhelmed). The Bible in this verse (Job 41:9) says "**even at the sight**". By this we also know that the 666-beast can't be any human US president nor a human Pope.

6. Job 41:10 **No one** is so fierce that he dares to stir him up. Who then is he who can stand before **me**?

   a. Who do you think the Bible is talking about when it says "**No one**", in Job 41:10? That's right, it means no one. Yahweh is talking to Job in this verse and Yahweh compares himself to Leviathan. God is basically saying, if no one is fierce enough to stir up Leviathan, then who can stand before me. What if God said to Job something like...[since no one is fierce enough to stir up a *(crocodile)*, then who could possibly stand before me]. From 1996 to 2007, there was a TV show called "The Crocodile Hunter", where a human would not only stir up a crocodile but he would also capture them to relocate them farther away from populated areas or into crocodile sanctuaries. So is it safe to say that this "Crocodile Hunter" can stand before God and therefore proved God wrong in Job 41:10. If you were a fan of the TV show ("The Crocodile Hunter"), then you know that the crocodile hunter was more than fierce enough to stir up massive crocodiles. What I just said in this paragraph is just as ludicrous as scholars claiming that Leviathan is just a crocodile (or any other animal of the commonly known animal kingdom). Or what if God said ...[since no one is fierce enough to stir up a (*mythological being*), then who could possibly stand before me]. Where it says (*mythological being*), just fill in that blank with all the options that scholars give us in their effort to avoid having to explain that a real seven headed dragon actually exists (i.e. crocodile, whale, elephant, hippopotamus, etc). It might be hard to believe that the ancient past is filled with incredibly fantastic things that we can't wrap our heads around...but the Bible is true and accurate. Leviathan is not a myth and he's not a mere animal from the commonly known animal kingdom. He is so intensely fearsome, he is literally a beast.

b. If Leviathan is merely a crocodile or merely a zoo animal, it is difficult to see why so much is made of him.

7. Job 41:18 **His sneezings flash forth light**, and his eyes are like the eyelids of the dawn.

    a. For some people, no matter what they see in their Bible, they will never believe that any real dragon ever existed. Come on people, his sneezings flashed forth light. How do you get the Roman Empire from that? The 666-beast is not the Roman Empire nor any organization. Organizations don't sneeze and if they do they certainly don't flash forth light.

    b. Look, I get it, the Roman Empire might once again become a strong ruling government in the prophetic end times. But even if that happens, it doesn't mean that the Roman Empire is the beast that will rise up out of the sea. And the Roman Empire will not be the beast whose name or the number of his name will be put on peoples hand or forehead. Now, it could be said that the 666-beast will be the leader of the re-birthed Roman Empire. But the beast itself will not be a government nor any type of organization like the Vatican. The beast is Leviathan and Leviathan is a seven headed dragon that actually existed and still exists bound up in or under the depth of the sea to this very day. That is the current location of the beast.

8. Job 41:19 **Out of his mouth go flaming torches; sparks of fire** leap forth.

    a. What is this thing that God is describing to Job in this verse (Job 41:19)? Doesn't it seem possible that God is describing an actual real dragon to Job? So why do people think that God is not describing a real dragon? Is God describing a thing that never existed? Why would God

161

allocate so much of his holy word to the description of something that never existed? I'm not saying that Christians are not intelligent. The most intelligent people I've ever met are Christians. So how can it be that dragons are simply unbelievable to most Christians?

9. Job 41:20 **Out of his nostrils comes forth smoke, as from a boiling pot and burning rushes.**
   a. Smoke from his nostrils? How much more does God need to say in his holy scriptures before people stop thinking that the "antichrist" is Obama, Donald Trump, or the Pope? People, this is a dragon. Show me something IN THE BIBLE that convinces me that I should not take God's description of Leviathan literally. I DON'T CARE WHAT Augustine or Tertullian SAID NOR ANY OTHER HUMAN IN HISTORY. I ONLY CARE ABOUT THE WORDS OF GOD IN HIS HOLY SCRIPTURES, PERIOD. I should clarify what I mean when I say I don't care. I do care about what others say and think but never at the expense of the Bible.

10. Job 41:21 **His breath kindles coals, and a flame comes forth from his mouth.**
   a. If God was going to put symbolic metaphors in his holy word, why would he go on and on and on describing physical attributes that perfectly match other ancient writings about "mythological" dragons? What's with the obsession of dragon attributes?

b. What symbolic metaphor do pastors and scholars use to get rid of the fact that God used the word breath? And how do Bible teachers and preachers deal with the flame that comes forth from Leviathan's mouth? I can just hear some of the Bible teachers trying to wiggle their way out of this verse (Job 41:21)...pastors might say something like..."**well, God didn't mean a literal flame and he didn't literally mean that it came out of Leviathan's mouth, instead what God meant was blah blah blah**". Stop trying to bend the Bible folks. The Bible means what it says and it says what it means, PERIOD.

c. Anything that tells you not to take the Bible literally comes from outside the Bible. There's nothing in the word of God itself that tells us not to take the Bible literally. Keep in mind that this Leviathan episode occurred over five thousand years ago (before the flood). We are so far removed from those ancient days that it just seems unbelievable to us. Yet somehow, we find it easy to believe in T-Rex and other dinosaurs. The education system that is controlled by Satan taught us about the dinosaurs.

11. Job 41:33 **On earth** there is not his like, a **creature** without fear.

a. Revelation 13:4 says that when people see the beast, they will say of it "...Who is like the beast...". Nowhere on this planet is there a creature like Leviathan. In this verse (Job 41:33), Leviathan is called a creature NOT an empire nor a kingdom nor an organization...Leviathan is a creature created by God. In the Hebrew, it is even clearer that God

163

literally created Leviathan and nothing on planet Earth is equivalent to Leviathan.

12. Job 41:34 **He sees <u>everything</u> that is high he is <u>king</u> over <u>all</u> the <u>sons of pride</u>**

    a. I expect that the critics of this book might make a broad sweeping comment that will eliminate the book of Job from out of the canon. The critics might say something to make it easier for you to sweep Leviathan under the rug and pretend it doesn't matter that much. But the word of God tells us that Leviathan is king over ALL the sons of pride. The "sons of pride" are the fallen elohim. Leviathan is the king over ALL of them which helps explain why Satan voluntarily hands over all of Satan's own power and authority to Leviathan.

13. Psalm 74:13-14 **You divided the sea by your might; you <u>broke the heads</u> of the sea <u>monsters</u> on the waters. ¹⁴You <u>crushed the heads</u> of Leviathan; you gave him as food for the creatures of the wilderness.**

    a. In Revelation 13:3 it says "One of its <u>heads</u> seemed to have a **mortal wound**, but its mortal wound was healed, and the whole earth marveled as they followed <u>the beast</u>."

    b. Notice that in Revelation 13:3, it is talking about the beast that comes up out of the sea. And Revelation 13:1 tells us that this is the beast that rises up out of the sea having seven heads. By the way, the "<u>whole earth</u>" is not going to "<u>follow</u>" the Roman Empire. The more you believe the Bible the less likely it is that you'll believe that the Roman Empire is the 666-beast. Stop trying to come up with alternate and fancy interpretations. Just read

164

the word of God and believe it. Well, at least that's what you ought to do if you claim to be a Bible believing Christian.

14. Revelation 19:19-20 **And I saw the beast and the kings of the earth with their armies gathered to make war against him who was sitting on the horse and against his army. 20 And the beast was captured, and with it the false prophet who in its presence had done the signs by which he deceived those who had received the mark of the beast and those who worshiped its image. These two were thrown alive into the lake of fire that burns with sulfur**

    a. I agree, that some things in the Bible are not literal and instead are symbolic. Yet some things are both literal and symbolic. Prophecy is inherently unclear, ambiguous and nebulous. Just like the prophecy of the resurrection of Jesus Christ. Where in the Old Testament do you see a clear prediction of our lord's resurrection? You don't see that in the Old Testament. In hind sight it might seem like we do, but it's not there. I think if Satan had known that the resurrection was going to guarantee his defeat, he would NOT have pursued the death of Jesus Christ. So I believe that the Holy Bible intentionally does not reveal the end times prophecies in great clarity so that Satan would not be successful in his end times agenda. But as the time of the death and resurrection of Jesus drew near, the Israelites were told by Jesus himself that he would rise back up in three days. I think it's possible that Jesus told them in the nick of time such that Satan would not have enough time to try and change the plan that had been put into motion whereby Jesus would be murdered on the cross. By the time Jesus told his closest loved ones, Satan's plan was already too far progressed. And so it is with the return of Leviathan. Now is the time for us Christians to know the true identity of the 666-beast including his name and current location. Some Bible scholars (not all, but some) have already written about Leviathan being the 666-beast but no one has yet been able to make it widespread knowledge among Christian congregations. I ask you to help me spread this word by helping me get this book into as many hands as possible. Now is the time that the saints of the final days will fully awaken.

b. The highlighted word "**and**" in Rev 19:19 tells us that there are not only "kings" but also a beast. In other words, the beast is not the kings. It's talking about the kings AND the beast which confirms that there is a beast. The word "**captured**" (in Rev 19:20) provides more evidence that the beast is not a group of seven mountains. It just doesn't make sense that seven mountains would be "**captured**".

c. The words "**in its presence**" means that the signs were performed in the presence of some entity and that entity (as you can see by reading Rev 17) is the beast. Just use your own mind to read Rev 17 and you yourself will be able to tell that it doesn't make as much sense to think that the false prophet performed signs in the presence of the Roman Empire. It makes more sense that the false prophet performed the deceptive signs in the presence of someone, a being...a living entity.

d. Did you notice the word "**alive**" in Revelation 19:20? Because of that word, it becomes even more clear that the 666-beast is NOT the Roman empire nor anything that isn't alive.

e. I know that for most of this book, I have strongly urged you to take the Bible literally. Taking it literally is the safest route because when the Bible is not to be taken literally it becomes obvious. Sometimes the symbolism of the Bible involves a literal thing that serves as a symbol for multiple things. For example, in Revelation 17:1 there is a "prostitute". So when you first read that verse you should literally think of an actual human being that provides the service of sexual intercourse in exchange for money or other valuable things. In Revelation chapter 17 verses 7, 9, 15 and 18 you see the other pieces that together give us a clear explanation of the "prostitute". So after further studying of the Bible, we eventually see that the prostitute is not a literal single human being. So the way to know if something should not be taken literally is by reading the rest of the specific book in the Bible that is in question (and sometimes more than just that single book). The context that surrounds that verse will let you know whether it is literal, symbolic or both. It will make it very clear just like Revelation chapter 17 makes it clear that the prostitute is not a literal "prostitute" in the common sense of that word. But always start with the assumption that it is literal until the context **FORCES** you to see it as something other than literal. If you read the entire Bible this way (i.e. literally), the whole Bible story starts to come into a more clear focus and many things that were previously ambiguous will suddenly make perfect sense. The Bible means what it says and it says what it means.

So after reading this book, it should be evident that there is no such thing as thee one main antichrist. And it should also be clearer that Satan himself is behind the misdirection. The Bible never refers to the beast as the antichrist. Not even one time does the Bible refer to the beast as the antichrist? I know I'm repeating myself here but where do people get the idea that the 666-beast is the antichrist. Satan is the deceiver who has been causing congregations to be on the lookout for something that does not exist (i.e. the coming antichrist). I think it's better for Satan's agenda if humans are caught off-guard and totally surprised by the seven-headed dragon of ancient historical record. The vast majority of Bible verses that are about Leviathan (i.e. the 666-beast) are literal and clear. Only a small minority of verses about the 666-beast use representative language or symbolism. For example;

Revelation 17:9-11
⁹ This calls for a **mind with wisdom**: the **seven heads** are seven **mountains** on which the woman is seated; ¹⁰ they are **also seven kings**, five of whom have fallen, one is, the other has not yet come, and when he does come he must remain only a little while. ¹¹ **As for the beast** that was and is not, it is an eighth but it belongs to the seven, and it goes to destruction

Verse 9 is telling us that an average ordinary mind will not be sufficient because it calls for a "mind with wisdom". Verse 9 also confirms that not all minds have wisdom. Therefore, what John wrote here is not simple to understand otherwise God would not have told us that it requires a mind with wisdom. The seven mountains are not the seven literal

168

heads of Leviathan so this is symbolic and representative. Furthermore, the fact that the seven heads are ALSO seven kings helps us to realize that this is talking in symbolic, metaphoric or representative language. Here's what I mean. If someone makes the following hypothetical statement;

"The disabled veterans that are homeless would not be homeless if Washington DC handled things differently."

Regarding Washington DC in the above statement, what comes to mind first for many readers of the above statement is the human being that holds the office of President in the USA. People don't read that statement and think that the physical City itself is being addressed here. Washington DC is a region of earthly terrain that is marked out by formal boundaries with streets, sidewalks and landscaping. Even though that geographic area is referred to as Washington DC, the above statement is not about a geographic area. It's about a human being. And it's whichever human being is the President at the time that statement was made.

The 666-beast appears to be another nebulous and ungraspable concept because the above verses (Revelation 17:9-11) refer to the seven heads as mountains. But you can't stop reading there. The seven heads are not just mountains for they are also Kings. This automatically should cause you to realize that this portion of the Bible is clueing us in on the idea that Leviathan will have a headquarters of sorts. I have reason to believe that the seven kings will be elohim (angels) and not human. Furthermore, in that geographic area of those seven mountains, there is a governing structure that involves seven kings. So the 666-beast (a.k.a. Leviathan), is a dragon that has seven literal heads but the number of heads is perhaps a prophetic type that represents the seven mountains from which it will govern the world with the help of seven kings. The seven kings represent leadership roles. You've heard phrases like, "he is the head of that department". And the beast belongs to the group of seven kings and is an eight king (in this case it's talking about the second beast, the angel named Apollyon).

Here's another example of what I call representative language.

Revelation 17:14
¹⁴ **They will make war on the <u>Lamb</u>, and the <u>Lamb</u> will conquer them, for he is Lord of lords and King of kings, and those with him are called and chosen and faithful.**

In the above verse, we know that the Lamb is not literally a white-wool animal with four legs. Revelation 17:14 does not tell us that the Lamb in this verse is Jesus Christ but we know that it is Jesus. We know it is Jesus because other parts of the Bible refer to Jesus as "Lord of Lords" and "King of Kings" (see Rev 19:11-16). However, the only ones that were saved from the death angel in the Exodus were those where God could see the blood of a lamb on the entrance into their dwellings. So there was an actual literal lamb and actual literal blood and actual literal salvation all during the time of the Exodus. The Passover narrative in the book of Exodus was a prophetic representation of Jesus, the Lamb whose blood was shed to save us. And representative language is what we find in Revelation 17:9-11

We are allowed to use our brain. We are not required to have others tell us what the Bible means. We can read it with our own eyes and we ought to. I recommend that you carefully study the Bible yourself. There's nothing wrong with listening to our pastors, preachers and Bible teachers. However, nothing outside the Bible is as accurate as the Bible itself because it's the word of God himself...the Holy Bible.

Earlier in this chapter we looked at the Hebrew word אלים and below is a table that helps to study that word. Table 13.1 below shows the only four times that this word occurs in the Bible. It's important for the Bible student to clearly see the proof that elim (אלים) means a powerful supernatural being that is non-human. That's because Job 41:25 is saying that the angels are beside themselves when Leviathan raises himself up which causes the sound of crashing. The elim are mighty supernatural beings some of which are called angels or elohim or gods or son's of God. This helps to prove that Leviathan is not a crocodile, nor a hippo nor a nonexistent mythological being.

Table 13.1

Biblia Hebreica Stuttgartensia (See chapter 4 for more about this Masoretic text)	ESV
Job 41:25 מִשֵּׂתוֹ יָגוּרוּ **אֵלִים** מִשְּׁבָרִים יִתְחַטָּאוּ׃	Job 41:25 When he raises himself up **the mighty** are afraid; at the crashing they are beside themselves
Daniel 11:36 וְעָשָׂה כִרְצוֹנוֹ הַמֶּלֶךְ וְיִתְרוֹמֵם וְיִתְגַּדֵּל עַל־כָּל־**אֵל** וְעַל אֵל אֵלִים יְדַבֵּר נִפְלָאוֹת וְהִצְלִיחַ עַד־כָּלָה זַעַם כִּי נֶחֱרָצָה נֶעֱשָׂתָה	Daniel 11:36 And the king shall do as he wills. He shall exalt himself and magnify himself above every god, and shall speak astonishing things against the God of **gods.** He shall prosper till the indignation is accomplished; for what is decreed shall be done.
Psalms 89:6 כִּי מִי בַשַּׁחַק יַעֲרֹךְ לַיהוָה יִדְמֶה לַיהוָה בִּבְנֵי **אֵלִים**	Psalms 89:6 For who in the skies can be compared to the LORD? Who among **the heavenly beings** is like the LORD
Psalms 29:1 הָבוּ לַיהוָה בְּנֵי **אֵלִים** הָבוּ לַיהוָה כָּבוֹד וָעֹז׃	Psalms 29:1 Ascribe to the LORD, **O heavenly beings,** ascribe to the LORD glory and strength

Table 13.1 above is important because it supports the analysis of Job 41:25 (see the 2nd verse analyzed above). The table proves that the only four times when the word אלים (elim) is used it always means non-humans of the divine supernatural realm. That also makes sense because the first two letters of the word are EL, which means god or mighty supernatural being. EL literally means the "powerful strong leader". Compare the word elohim to the word elim. And then compare that to eilm.

אלהים = (elohim) gods

אלים = (elim) the mighty, gods, or heavenly beings

אילם = (eilm) ram; notice the "L" and the "I" are transposed

The reason I'm spending some time on the word elim and the word eilm is because I want you to see how easy it would be to transpose those two letters in error. Or maybe not in error but rather like the word Easter in the King James Version wherein it was intentionally to mislead. Well, in the Masoretic text, I'm not sure if it was intentionally to mislead or by error or even perhaps due to a bias that might have been inherent in the theology of the Masoretic Jews...but however it happened, the Masoretic Text has an error in Exodus 36:19 where the word אלים (elim) was used in the Masoretic Text when it should have obviously been the word אילם (eilm).

All English translations translate אלים to the word ram in Exodus 36:19. That provides additional proof that the Masoretic Text should have had "eilm" and not "elim" there. Keep in mind that the Masoretic Text was written circa seventh through tenth century AD while the Dead Sea Scrolls were written around 1 to 3 centuries BC. Compare that to the autograph of Exodus which was written circa 16th century BC, which is when Jesus helped Moses split the sea to help the Israelites have a successful exodus out of Egypt. And, the Masoretic Text was written largely from the memory of the Masoretic Jews. If Satan was trying to keep Christians blindfolded and if he wanted to hide the identity of the 666-beast, it would make a lot of sense for him to try to dilute the word elim and confuse it with the word eilm because then Satan could try to weaken the message of Job 41:25.

Most orthodox Jews don't put too much weight on the Masoretic Text because it is owned and controlled by the Germans. Today, the Masoretic Text is known as the "Biblia Hebreica Stutgartensia" because it is administered out of Stuttgart Germany. Remember that the Germans were the ones that tried to eliminate the Jewish descendants of Abraham, Isaac and Jacob in the Jewish holocaust under the leadership of Hitler.

In the entire Old Testament, the word אילם (eilm) occurs twenty five (25) times in that exact format and that exact spelling (i.e. eilm). All 25 times. it is translated into the word "ram". Conversely, the word אלים occurs only four times in the Bible. It is pronounced elim or alim and all for times it means non-humans of the divine supernatural realm. We don't count Exodus 36:19 as a fifth time due to the typo explained above.

The myths about dragons have traveled worldwide more so than other myths. Dragon myths have reach more ancient civilizations than even vampires. Dragons turn up in cultures and civilizations so far apart in time and space that it seems

174

impossible. Dragons are in the ancient Sumerian tablets, they are in the Ugaritic tablets, they're in the Mayan ruins, they're in China, the Norse and Christian mythologies, the ancient Jewish literature has dragons. And the ancient Greeks would be insulted if they could see us modern Americans call their literature a myth. They certainly didn't write it as if it was myth. The Greeks are not the only ancients that would be insulted, all of those ancient writings wrote it down as if they were recording historical fact. As recent as 120 years ago, Victorian scientists wrote that dragons had once existed but they had gone extinct.

For me, the Bible is enough proof. That is all I need…the Bible, the word of God.

May Jesus Christ of Nazareth bless you and keep your name in the Book of Life.

Chapter 14

☼ **Some Parting Thoughts**

- The son of perdition = one destined for destruction, to be destroyed or to cause destruction.
- The lawless one or the man of lawlessness. Gabriel is called "the man Gabriel" (Daniel 9:21). So when angels are called "man" in the Bible, it doesn't mean that they're not an angel. The non-human elohim that ate with Abraham were not human yet they were called men. Therefore, it's a weak argument to say that the beasts in Revelation are human if one of those beasts is called the man of lawlessness.
- The book of Enoch found among the Dead Sea Scrolls uses the term lawless man or the man of lawlessness in reference to an elohim.
- The 666-beast is never called the antichrist.
- The word beast is in reference to any flesh and blood that isn't Gods original human creation. Humans are never called "beast".
- The 2nd beast is non-human making it more plausible that the 1st beast is also non-human.
- According to the Bible (except for the two witnesses dressed in black...which may be human), all the major players having a significant role in the end-time wars are elohim. In the minds of many American Christians the only one that is not elohim is the 666-beast.
- What is it that Obama is going to do that is going to cause the WHOLE WORLD to worship him?

- The sea-beast has seven heads in revelation and during the time of the OT writing, the contemporaries were aware that the sea-beast had seven heads, it went without saying back then. Just like today, when we mention the Pope, we would not need to clarify that we're talking about the one that is "in the Vatican".

Contact Me

I'd love to hear from you. And I'd love to be a guest speaker at your church. So please ask your pastor to read this book (I'll send him a free copy). Ask your pastor to contact me so he and I can arrange for me to speak at your church.

Please don't hesitate to email me directly at

domenechhg@gmail.com

or visit my website

www.TheAntichristRevealed.com

I am also available to speak at any venue (not just churches). So just contact me directly to have me as a guest speaker.

Check my website periodically for updates and information about my next book.

Made in the USA
Middletown, DE
11 September 2020